THE BLACK WIDOW

Also by Kate Kray

Hard Bastards
Hard Bastards 2
The Twins: Free at Last
Killers

THE BLACK WIDOW

The Life and Crimes of
LINDA CALVEY

KATE KRAY and **CHESTER STERN**

headline

First published in 2002
by HEADLINE BOOK PUBLISHING

10 9 8 7 6 5 4 3 2 1

Cataloguing in Publication Data is available from the British Library

Text design by The Flying Fish

Typeset in Baskerville by Avon Dataset Ltd, Bidford-on-Avon, Warks

ISBN 0 7553 1035 7

Printed and bound in Great Britain by
Mackays of Chatham plc, Chatham, Kent

HEADLINE BOOK PUBLISHING
A division of Hodder Headline
338 Euston Road
London NW1 3BH

www.headline.co.uk
www.hodderheadline.com

CONTENTS

INTRODUCTION

Gangster, armed robber, murderer – not terms usually associated with a woman, but Linda Calvey is not just any woman. She is the only female gangster in this country. She is also an armed robber and at the moment she is serving a life sentence for murder.

Towards the end of the twentieth century British criminologists began to note that women were moving out from what had been seen as their traditional role, supporting their brothers, fathers and lovers in the commission of crime, into independent criminal operator status in their own right.

Among academics it became almost politically incorrect to suggest that women criminals were dependent upon men for their livelihood. Many observers felt that women could and should be as bad as, or worse, than their male counterparts.

In recent times sociologists, too, have identified a growing trend towards violent crime in the female population – a trend they attribute to greater emancipation and a realignment of the female place in society.

The social commentator Jeannette Kupferman wrote: 'It might be seen as the logical outcome of women being encouraged to be more assertive, more independent, and more equal – and thinking they have to be more equal in aggression, too – a sort of perverse equality. The logical outcome of doing away with the feminine stereotype of submissiveness, gentleness, empathy and caring – the devaluation of woman as peacemaker.

'The distorted thinking that says if we are going to be more like men and share in their power, we have to stop reasoning and hit out. Somewhere along the line self-assertion has been confused with the often disastrous expression of raw anger.'

Be that as it may, the worldwide history of crime is littered with the stories of formidable women. However, the record of women in gangland is rare. They are usually minders of property, cheque fraudsters, providers of alibis, and regular visitors to prisons.

Throughout the eighties there were persistent rumours of women who actually went 'over the pavement' on armed robberies, but only one woman stood out as queen of the sawn-off shotgun – the toughest and most fearless of them all.

That woman was Linda Calvey, Britain's first and only female gangster – a gangster's moll who became more dangerous than the men who fell beneath her spell.

Dubbed 'The Black Widow' – the female spider which devours its partner after mating – this glamorous grandmother, whose once-intoxicating beauty remains spell-binding, retains an insatiable appetite for men. Her sinister nickname was coined after the death of her first husband, who was gunned down by the Flying Squad while carrying out an armed robbery, when one detective said: 'Every man she has had a relationship with is either dead or serving a long prison sentence.'

Her remarkable life and extraordinary criminal escapades, she claims, were the inspiration behind the smash-hit TV series *Widows* about a group of women who launched a campaign of armed robberies while their gangster husbands were in jail. Writer Lynda la Plante, who interviewed Calvey while researching the storylines, denies that the main character, Dolly Rawlins, was based directly on her. There are, however, uncanny echoes of Linda's life elsewhere in the series. One of the main characters, like Calvey, shoots dead her lover, and one of the characters is called Linda.

Not only is Calvey, as a woman robber, unique in the underworld, but almost every male who came into contact with her became entangled in her web and was eventually brought down.

First it was Micky Calvey – the flashy armed robber from the East End whose life was cut short by a policeman's bullet. Then there was Ronnie Cook – a tough, violent gangster jailed for his part in a £1 million heist. He introduced her to Brian Thorogood – her minder and, later, her lover. Finally there was Danny Reece – the hitman she hired who couldn't bring himself to kill . . . so she had to pull the trigger herself.

Along the way there were proposals of marriage from Reg Kray and prison hardman Charlie Bronson.

Love her or loathe her, Linda Calvey is a woman not to be ignored. There is no doubt that men find her irresistible, but for some who fell under the Black Widow's spell it turned out to be the ultimate fatal attraction.

I first met Linda seven years ago while researching my book *Lifers* – a series of interviews with prisoners serving life sentences. The book was an attempt to probe the minds, personalities and motivations of killers incarcerated for years on end with little prospect of a future life outside the prison walls. As a woman who had grown used to the attitudes and peculiar mores of male gangsters I wanted to include a woman in my researches – to discover what might drive a member of the gentler sex, my own sex, to compete with the men in violent crime, to commit cold-blooded brutal murder, and to cope with an almost endless future behind bars.

I had heard the legend of Linda Calvey on the underworld grapevine and I was intrigued, so I wrote to her in the top-security H Wing women's section of Durham Prison. Perhaps because of my name she agreed to see me.

I was not prepared for what I would find. The platinum blonde hair had gone, to be replaced by a soft shade of chestnut. Still a beautiful woman, she spoke with a gentle but persuasive tone. She entertained me with tea from her best china tea service and we became firm friends.

Ever since that first encounter I have visited Linda two or three times a month. We correspond regularly and chat on the telephone frequently. I confess that I find her fascinating if at times a little chilling. Hardened criminals used to melt at the sound of her voice or the look in her eyes and it is an uncanny quality she still possesses. I have seen male visitors and male prison staff embarrassingly captivated by her. She undoubtedly has a mesmeric quality which even I, as a woman, find compelling.

She talks about her crimes in a bland matter-of-fact way without a hint of melodrama. She is not crude or foul-mouthed. Her conversation is refined, almost genteel. There is no remorse yet no triumphalism either, certainly no sense of adrenaline rush or glory-seeking. It is almost as though, for her, the criminal way of life is the norm. She also seems to accept the notion that prison is the natural consequence of law-breaking. Although she still firmly maintains her innocence it is not an obsession and she never appears to be unduly sorry for herself.

Visiting Linda is an extraordinary experience. But for the drab surroundings of a prison visitors' room you could be forgiven for imagining that you were taking tea with a titled lady in the drawing room of a stately home.

Her clothes are elegant and expensive, her make-up immaculate and her hair always beautifully coiffeured. She always sits erect, her back straight, her head tilted slightly and her knees carefully crossed.

Food – tiny sandwiches, cakes and chocolates – is presented on paper doilies and served to her guests on bone china plates. Every mouthful she takes is followed by a delicate dabbing of the corners of her mouth with a linen napkin.

She is acutely aware of her place in British criminal folklore and has a keen eye for the grand gesture which will maintain her reputation and attract publicity. In this connection it was no surprise to me that, when she was preparing to wed Danny Reece behind bars, she asked to borrow the dress I had worn for my Broadmoor marriage to Ronnie Kray.

There is little doubt that the prison service is intimidated by Linda Calvey. She has been called many names in her time from Lavender Lady (the name she chose to put on her first husband's funeral wreath) to The Black Widow and even The Black Rose – a nickname given to her by Charlie Bronson. In prison, however, she is known simply as 'Ma' – a term not so much of affection for a protective motherly figure but more of fear for the matriarch who intimidates all around her – inmates and staff alike – with the sheer force of her manipulative and malevolent personality.

Over the years I have listened and become both enthralled and horrified by Linda's remarkable story.

This is my distillation of what she has to say about the part she played in armed robberies. She talks frankly about murder and sex and about her life behind bars where she rubs shoulders with the likes of Moors Murderess Myra Hindley and House of Horrors killer Rose West among dozens of the most callous, ruthless and cold-blooded females in British criminal history.

Now fifty-three, and eleven years into the life sentence from which she hopes to win parole, Linda talks movingly about what it was like, after a respectable law-abiding upbringing, to be plunged by a quirk of fate into a mind-boggling life of crime.

Even though she is not being paid a penny, she has urged me to write this book – spending hours recording reminiscences over classical music tapes and writing copious notes detailing the minutiae of her lavish spending sprees and numerous romantic encounters.

Linda hopes that this book will establish her innocence and hasten her release from jail. She may not like what it reveals about the true nature of the Black Widow.

Kate Kray
London
July 2002

1

'KNEEL!'

It was an ordinary suburban kitchen. On the draining board lay a haphazard jumble of pots, pans and crockery. An electric kettle and a pop-up toaster were tucked neatly into the corner of the work surface. Two damp tea towels were draped casually over the cutlery tray.

A wholly unremarkable domestic scene.

Unremarkable, that is, except for the blood. Except for the blood and the smell.

Shards of glass from a shattered milk bottle lay scattered across the grey tiled floor. The puddle of milk was tinged with pink at the edges.

A crimson stain of blood was splashed across the blue cupboard doors, splaying upwards in a starburst pattern. The neat blue and white gingham curtains were dappled with a fine spray of tiny red spots.

The ceiling and the light fitting were festooned with glistening glutinous lumps of varying hues – a mixture of skin, flesh, hair and fragments of skullbone.

In the middle of the floor, and spreading slowly, was a pool of rich dark-red fresh blood.

At the centre of the pool lay the body of a man. A big man.

His legs were tucked under him awkwardly where he had been blasted backwards from a kneeling supplicant position. A darker stain seeped through the chest of his sky-blue bomber jacket.

His head was almost unrecognisable as human. His tongue lolled grotesquely on his chin and an eyeball hung crazily from its shattered socket. The rest was an indistinguishable mess of pulp.

The air was heavy with the choking, acrid smell of cordite.

For a moment this grisly scene seemed frozen in time.

The silence was broken by a globule of grey brain tissue which slithered down the tiled wall and dropped into the sink with an eerie plop.

Then from somewhere deep in the woman's throat came a sound. It started as a strangled gurgle, then a low moan, and finally a long piercing scream – a cascade of unintelligible words tumbling over one another in a single agonised howl.

The dead man was Ronald Cook, one of the most notorious gangsters in British criminal history.

The woman was his long-time gangster's moll, Linda Calvey, and the bloody carnage was all of her making.

Moments earlier the cold-eyed platinum blonde had callously ordered her lover to his knees before she literally blew him away with a sawn-off shotgun.

She had not intended it to be that way.

She had placed a contract on Cook's head in the time-honoured fashion of the underworld, but the courage of the hitman she had paid £10,000 to do the job had failed him at the crucial moment. So the 42-year-old mother of two had grabbed the gun and calmly completed the execution herself. A year later the whole chilling tale, in all its gory detail, was told to the historic Number One court of the Old Bailey.

The jury heard that Calvey was the classic gangster's moll – hard, coarse, yet dressed in the finest furs. She was reputed to act as an 'armourer' for robbers by hiding a stock of guns and ammunition for them. The men in her life, and there had been many, were, nearly all, villains: brutal, uncaring, greedy men but infatuated with Calvey on whom they would lavish attention, money and luxuries.

She had been dubbed 'The Black Widow' during a high-profile campaign she waged against the police after her first husband, armed robber Michael Calvey, was shot dead by detectives while making his getaway from a raid.

She was, said the prosecution, 'in her chosen sphere a woman of some influence. She is not a quiet, put-upon woman under the influence of domineering men but a woman attractive to, and attracted by, armed robbers.'

After Michael Calvey's death Linda was befriended by Cook, another armed robber always suspected of being part of the same gang, and began to live a millionaire lifestyle on the proceeds of his criminal activities. While his long-suffering wife could barely afford the price of a winter coat, Cook showered his mistress with money and gifts, taking her on holidays to Las Vegas where they watched Muhammad Ali's last fight and once blew £30,000 in eight days in casinos.

On one occasion Cook even gave Linda £4,000 for plastic surgery to reduce her waistline.

The good life came to an abrupt end when Cook was jailed for sixteen years for his part in an £800,000 armed robbery described at his trial as 'one of the most spectacular and well-planned robberies in the history of crime'. Calvey promised to wait for him. She had

'True Love Ron Cook' tattooed on her leg, and Cook arranged for a friend, Brian Thorogood, another robber, to look after his mistress while he was inside.

Thorogood took to his task too well, however, and soon became Linda's lover. He left his wife and bought a house for the couple to live together.

By now Calvey was dipping into Cook's nest egg, spending the money he had hidden and keeping her deception and the affair with Thorogood a secret during her visits to see Cook in jail.

She embarked on her own criminal escapades and was eventually jailed for seven years for conspiracy to rob. Thorogood was jailed for twenty-one years at the same trial.

On her release the duplicitous Calvey had two villains to visit in prison – Cook and Thorogood – assuring both her lovers of her enduring affections.

As Cook was nearing the end of his sentence and the time for his release approached she became terrified that he would try to kill her when he discovered her two-timing and the theft of his ill-gotten gains. There are stories that Cook had formerly treated her badly – beating her up and subjecting her to sadistic sexual practices.

Linda determined that there was only one solution to her complicated set of circumstances. Cook had to be eliminated.

Trying to find someone to kill him was not easy, however. Most of her numerous underworld contacts were either friends of Cook or afraid of him, so she hatched a plan. She travelled to the Verne Prison in Dorset to visit Daniel Reece, a 35-year-old friend of Thorogood's who was coming to the end of his sentence.

Unpopular with fellow inmates, Reece fell easy prey to Calvey's charms. As they sat drinking tea beneath the noses of the prison guards she coolly offered him £10,000 to assassinate Cook.

Reece was instantly infatuated with Calvey and readily agreed to carry out the job while on weekend release. However, unlike the professional killers who had already turned the contract down, Reece had no experience of cold-blooded murder.

On the agreed date Calvey collected Reece from prison and drove him to London. She gave him the choice of two sawn-off shotguns hidden beneath the floorboards of her house and gave him a key.

The following day she collected 56-year-old Cook from Maidstone Prison where he had special permission to leave the jail during the day. He was supposed to remain nearby but made the unofficial trip to London expecting to spend the day in his lover's arms. Instead she first took him to an East End pub, ironically called The Widow's Son, so that Reece could identify his target.

As the couple eventually arrived at her house in London's docklands, Reece was lying in wait wearing a black tracksuit and white baseball cap. He burst in behind them, armed with Calvey's shotgun, and fired once. Then he panicked. He told police:

'I aimed the gun but at the last minute I shot to the side hitting him in the elbow. He fell backwards into the kitchen. I moved forward and stood over him and again aimed the gun but I froze. I could not kill him. I have never killed anyone. Linda grabbed the gun from me. She screamed at him "Kneel!" She pointed the gun at him. They spoke to each other. Then Linda just shot him in the head. She yelled at me to get out of the house.'

Reece made his way to Waterloo station and managed to return to the Verne Prison without initially arousing suspicion.

That was the story that the prosecution laid before the Old Bailey judge and jury during a sensational four-week trial.

However, perhaps not surprisingly, Linda Calvey herself gives an alternative version of events leading up to the killing and, in her own words, paints a wholly different picture of the fateful day itself:

It wasn't like the police and the papers tried to make out. They said that Ron had the needle about me seeing Brian. That wasn't the case at all. For a start I could never have had the affair with Brian if

Ron hadn't given his approval. What Ron had the hump about was that Brian got me nicked.

While I was completing my sentence I was able to visit Ron every three months and eventually he was moved to Maidstone Prison in Kent. Soon after that I was moved to Cookham Wood prison, also in Kent.

All the time I was writing to both Ron and Brian. I was mixed up. I didn't want to let Ron down – or Brian. And then there was Danny . . .

Through letters we had become very close. I told him that I felt he'd become like a brother to me. There was a special bond between us. I'd ask his advice and he'd ask mine. He told me how he and his wife had split up and all about his three sons.

While he was in prison his eldest son had been run over and killed and Danny was distraught. I felt sad for him and shared his sorrow through our regular letters. By a strange coincidence his son was buried in the same cemetery as my Micky, just 200 yards away. I promised Danny that when I was released I would put some flowers on the boy's grave for him. I tried to comfort him. I told him, 'He'll know they're from you.'

When I was released I continued to visit Ron in Maidstone Prison. I did not visit Brian but went to see Danny instead. I fulfilled my promise and put flowers on his son's grave. That made him happy.

I told Ron all about visiting Danny but he didn't mind because he had much more important things on his mind. He was on his way out and had a job cleaning the hostel attached to the prison. Once he had finished his cleaning duties he had the rest of the day to himself and did not have to return to prison until eight o'clock in the evening. He would ring me and we would go for a drink or a meal or, as increasingly happened, I would bring him to my home.

Ron didn't have much longer to serve. He was due out on 19 December 1990. He had left his money with 'friends' to look after but now he was coming home he wanted it back. That wasn't so easy. The 'friends' he'd left it with wouldn't, or couldn't, give it back to him.

Ron was furious and swore vengeance if his dough was not returned to him. The London underworld was awash with rumour. Ron was a formidable force and no one was in any doubt that he would wreak havoc if his money was not given back – to the last penny.

His temporary bankers were in a corner, they had little choice, they either had to give Ron his money back – or kill him.

Danny had moved to the Verne Prison at Portland, Dorset and I went to visit him. He was so happy. He'd just learned that he'd been granted home leave and the first thing he was going to do was catch a train and visit his son's grave.

I knew how upset he was over the boy. I couldn't let him catch a train and go on his own so I insisted on taking him. I also knew that he didn't have any up-to-date clothes to wear when he came out of prison and I knew from personal experience exactly how embarrassing that could be. So I bought him a black suede jacket and a smashing silk shirt. He was choked up when I gave them to him. Danny is a proud man and found it hard to accept them from me. I told him they were a gift but he insisted that he would pay me back when he got out and got himself straight.

On the Friday morning that Danny was coming home I was very excited and got up early for my long drive down to Dorset. I picked up my friend Ashley on the way as she had agreed to come along for company.

It was a freezing-cold November day and we sat outside the prison with the car heater full on and wiping the steam from the windscreen with our woolly gloves.

When we saw Danny come out of the big gate we both jumped out of the car and gave him a big kiss and a cuddle. It was good to see him free for the first time since I had met him.

We stopped on the way for breakfast and again to pick up a wreath. When we got to the cemetery Danny was beside himself with grief. He threw himself on top of the grave and sobbed as though his heart would break.

I was choked. I didn't know what to say. I had no words to comfort him. Ashley and I walked back to the car to wait for him. He seemed to stay at the grave forever. When he got back into the car none of us spoke. I drove him to his mother's house in silence.

I asked if he would like to go out that evening but he said that all he wanted was a home-cooked roast dinner. So Ashley and I bought a chicken and prepared a meal for him. We all had a drink and a lovely evening and that is how Danny's fingerprints came to be in my house – just three people enjoying each other's company, nothing more sinister as the police later tried to make out.

On the Sunday morning I had just come back from buying shellfish for tea from Chapel Market when the phone rang. It was Ron.

'Fancy a drink, Darling?' he asked.

Ronnie was always great company so I quickly agreed to meet him later at his favourite pub. He was already at the bar when I arrived and we had a super afternoon drinking and laughing together. It was just brilliant and when Ron told me that he was being allowed out again the following day I suggested that I pick him up from the prison first thing.

We left the pub at four o'clock and his nephew drove Ron back to Maidstone while I set off home.

The next morning Ron was waiting at the prison gates when I drove up. He waved, then ran back inside and came out with a big bag of personal photographs that I had sent him over the years. They'd been all over the walls of his cell but he was coming home for good two weeks later so he had been clearing out the cell ready for his release. As he got in the car he kissed me and we drove off. Halfway home we stopped for petrol and Ron took over the driving while I looked through the photographs and reminisced about the good times we'd enjoyed together. We were really in good spirits.

In the pub the day before he'd asked me what I wanted for Christmas and cheekily I'd asked for a Mercedes sports car the same as Princess Diana's. His nephew was very put out that I'd been so demanding but Ron just laughed. 'If that's what you want, baby, that's what you're getting,' he chuckled.

As we drove back to London I added: 'Don't forget that you also promised that if I waited for you I'd get a special loyalty present. Here I am, I've waited for you, so what about it?'

'Yeah, I know, what do you want?' he asked.

'I want a three-carat diamond ring,' I replied and as I thumbed through the photographs I added, 'And don't forget, when you get my car sorted out I want black, first choice, silver, second choice, or if not, white.'

Ron roared his head off.

'Yes, madam,' he said, 'and what if I can only get you a blue one?'

'You'll have to have it resprayed then won't you,' I said.

'You are a flash bitch,' he giggled.

'And I want a blue white diamond three-carat solitaire,' I added.

'Yes, madam. Anything else?' he asked. It was a lovely funny drive we had together that day.

Three months earlier I had bought a little black Orion Ghia car, nothing very special.

'Actually you can let me have this car in exchange,' said Ron.

That was typical of him because for all his money he was never flash. He was very conservative in his style of clothes – very sombre. He never wore jewellery or even a watch and always drove a nondescript car because he didn't want to draw attention to himself. He told me that I was his shop window and that was why he lavished everything on me.

In many ways our relationship was quite unconventional – but then all my relationships have been unconventional. I have always chosen strong men, powerful men. They've all been keep-fit fanatics and all very attractive. The other thing they've all had in common is that they've all loved me, all spoilt me and all doted on me – Ron probably more than anybody.

He often said that he'd made at least three fortunes by being an armed robber. In fact he was so rich that he didn't have to rob anymore. I think he only did the last one, where he got caught, just for the buzz – unlike Micky who did the robbery that he died on out of desperation.

Where I lived at the time was a bit off the beaten track; you had to approach it through a number of little back streets and tight turnings.

Just before we got to my street Ron suddenly pulled over to the side of the road. I asked what the matter was and he said: 'There's a motor following us', just as an electrician's van went past.

I said: 'He's not following. That's the electrician who lives at the end of my road. He always comes home for his dinner at this time – you really are paranoid.'

'Yeah, you better believe it, I am,' was all he said in reply.

My house was in a cul-de-sac facing a park. It was routine to drive to the end and turn round before parking outside the house. As Ron turned the car I noticed a man and two women unloading shopping on to the pavement and a policeman patrolling in the park.

Ron handed me the front door keys and I asked him to bring the milk in from the doorstep.

About two seconds later my life changed forever.

We had just walked into the kitchen when there was an almighty crash as the front door burst open. A big man rushed in. He was dressed all in black with the coat collar pulled up and a hat pulled right down over his face. All I could see were his eyes. He yelled: 'Get down, police!'

Ron turned and said: 'What's up, mate?'

In an instant the man fired, hitting Ron in the elbow and knocking him off balance. Ron staggered back into the kitchen in what seemed to me like slow motion. I didn't even see the gun. It was either in a bag or wrapped up in something.

I saw blood seeping through Ron's pale-blue bomber jacket and I screamed and put my hands over my face. Then I cowered in the corner. Within seconds I heard another deafening bang. I closed my eyes tight and hid my face because I was petrified. I didn't see the second shot, just a puff of smoke.

When I finally gained the courage to look up again the man had gone but there was a terrible hissing sound. Slowly I stood up, trying not to make a sound. I looked at Ron. He was covered in blood.

I was fighting for breath, just gasping for air. I ran towards the phone and then remembered the policeman in the park. The front door was wide open and I dashed out screaming my head off.

The three people I'd seen unloading shopping earlier came running over. I was hysterical and could only point to the house. One of the women was a nurse and she and the man rushed inside. I tried to tell the man what had happened, but I wasn't making any sense. I screamed at him to get the policeman in the park and he ran off to fetch him. The woman came out of the house and also ran off to tell the policeman that Ron was dead.

I went back inside in a daze. There was blood everywhere, my Ron's blood. He just lay there. Still, unrecognisable with half of his head missing.

In blind panic I screamed at him: 'Get up Ronnie! Get up!' but there was no movement. He was dead.

The next thing I remember was the policeman putting his arm around me and saying: 'It's okay dear, just take it easy.' Then he got on his radio and he said: 'It's 12.28. It's a murder.' It must have been one of the freshest scenes of a murder the police had ever come across. It had literally happened just moments earlier.

I was in a state of shock. I tried to answer the police questions as best I could. I told them everything I could remember but I had a mental block. It had all happened so quickly.

At first the police were very kind and considerate to me. They treated me as what I was – a deeply traumatised witness to murder. They made me a cup of coffee and arranged for my brother to collect fresh clothes for me, so that they could take my clothing away for forensic examination. They called a doctor to come and see me, and then invited me to do a test to see if I'd handled a gun or not. They offered me a solicitor to be present and to this day I could kick myself for not taking up that offer.

The detectives said: 'There are only two results to these tests, positive or negative. We expect them to be negative but you do realise that if they come back positive you could be charged with murder.'

I said: 'That's fine. I didn't do it. Please go ahead with the tests.'

A man came in with a little tray with bits and pieces on it and swabbed my face and my hands.

I only had tissues on me and they wanted a handkerchief for me to blow into. One of the detectives offered his handkerchief. It was folded, white with a blue initial on it. The officer said: 'It's not new but it is clean.'

The scientist said: 'That will do, but you won't get it back,' to which the policeman replied: 'That's all right. She's welcome to it.'

Anyway, sometime later the scientist came back and said: 'They're negative. She didn't do it.'

One of the detectives turned to me and said: 'We didn't expect the tests to be positive but it is good that you've had them done because it will clear up any doubt or confusion in the future.'

In fact the police did believe Linda's story in the early stages. Press reports based on information officially released from Scotland Yard spoke of 'an assassin posing as a policeman' and 'a gunman dressed in black'.

In court Linda was later to claim that the gunman had appeared in her kitchen and yelled: 'Get down, police,' or, somewhat unbelievably, 'Get down, please.'

One report, in the *Daily Mail*, spoke of the police having not ruled out a gangland vendetta relating to the original robbery for which Cook was jailed in 1981: 'Police believe the 56-year-old tailor may have been the victim of a gangland feud. Detective Superintendent Michael Morgan said yesterday: 'It bore all the hallmarks of an execution.'

However, the attitude of the murder squad detectives was soon to change. Linda's account continues:

I had made a full statement signed in my own name the following day but it wasn't until a few days later that the police discovered I was *the* Linda Calvey – the wife of Micky Calvey, the armed robber who had been shot by one of their own – the Linda Calvey who had kicked up such a stink about Micky's death.

Two and a half weeks after Ronnie was shot the police arrested me and charged me with murder. I couldn't believe it. Then they arrested Danny. They said he'd confessed that, together, we'd hatched the plan to kill Ron and that it was me who fired the fatal shot.

I knew that was nonsense. Danny wouldn't have said that. Why should he? But the police were adamant that I did it.

Later I discovered that the police had interviewed Danny in prison and he told them he'd never met Ron. He told them that he knew Ron was my long-time boyfriend and that I was looking forward to having him home after all those years. Nevertheless they charged Danny with murder too.

They didn't stop there. They accused Ashley's boyfriend Billy Francis of being the getaway driver. If it hadn't been so serious it would have been laughable – he only drove a Y-registered Yugo! They charged another man, Billy Swan. They even charged my daughter Melanie.

All these charges were later dropped, but they pressed the ones against Danny and me.

We were on remand for a year and once a month we had to appear in Stratford Magistrates Court in the East End. It is a very small court and you can't drive the vans in close. They park outside in the street and the prisoners have to walk across the pavement into the building and down to the cells. For me all this was quite nasty because there was a group of people who gathered outside the court every month to spit at me and scream 'Murdering Bitch!', 'Slag!', 'Whore!', and all kinds of foul abuse.

They seemed to feel sorry for Danny and often called out: 'You poor bastard. She's done you as well!'

I could understand their bitter feelings because many people were critical of the way Ron had abandoned his wife of twenty years and his children for me.

All of this dragged on for months until one day, after Danny had been taken away, I was brought out to find that the van which had earlier transported me to court was covered in graffiti. A hangman's noose had been spray-painted alongside the slogan: 'Inside this van is a murderess', and a host of obscenities. The driver and crew were horrified but could do nothing about it. On the way back to prison we seemed to stop at every traffic light and alongside every bus-stop and I was acutely aware that people were peering in through the windows trying to catch a glimpse of the 'murderess'. I was terribly embarrassed but I sat there trying to hold my head erect and avoid the eyes of the outside world while I wished for the relative safety of Holloway Prison.

That day we stopped on the way back at Highbury Court and picked up one girl. I think she was only a prostitute or something like that who was just remanded to Holloway for a couple of days.

She came out and said: 'Cor, look at the state of this van! I'm not getting in there, they'll think I'm a murderess.' Gesturing towards me she added: 'They must think the same about that poor woman in there.'

After that incident the lawyers all argued for a change of court and our case was transferred to Bow where there was total security.

During that period my family got together and offered half-a-million pounds as surety for bail – £250,000 in cash and £250,000 in bonds and securities. It was turned down because the police believed that I would abscond. That was simply ridiculous because I didn't do it so I would not have absconded if it was a few thousand pounds security.

I discussed the situation with my solicitor and my family. I've got a very large family of brothers and sisters and between them they've been very successful in business and property development over the years so they came up with one of the largest bail sureties ever offered – one million pounds. Again bail was refused, so it was off to Holloway to await my trial.

Arriving at the Old Bailey was also a daunting experience. The prison bus drives in to the yard and on to a huge turntable which rotates the vehicle through 180 degrees. It reminded me of one of those Swiss weather clocks where a little man or a little lady pops out either side to show whether it is going to be fine or wet – very strange. Every day as we went into court there were always lots of armed police everywhere – on the roof, in the corridors, wearing flak jackets and bristling with machine guns. All this security for little old me. If I hadn't been facing such serious charges I'd have found it all quite amusing.

The whole place is awfully intimidating. The steps up from the cells into the dock seem to go on for ever – clanging iron steps just going up and up and up.

One of the wooden chairs in the dock of Number One court has a notice on it saying 'Crippen Sat Here'. When I saw that I quipped to the warder: 'Oh God, Crippen sat here, that fills you with hope doesn't it?'

The dock officer replied, 'Not only Crippen, so did Lord Haw-Haw, and the Kray twins,' and he reeled off a whole list of names of famous criminals over the years.

I just giggled and asked: 'Can't you think of anyone who sat on that chair and was found not guilty?' We all fell about laughing because none of us really believed that I would be convicted.

The whole prosecution case revolved around the statements of my next-door neighbour, Mrs Saville, who testified that she heard a woman's voice shouting 'Oh no, Neil,' and then the sound of gunfire. She thought the voice belonged to me.

She went on to say that she looked out of the window and saw me talking to a man before he ran off towards the park. The second time she looked out she saw a policeman with two women and a man hurrying towards the house.

She was right. She did see all those things but they were misinterpreted in court.

The prosecution said I yelled 'Kneel! Kneel!' But Mrs Saville was right, I was shouting out 'Oh no, Neil!', which is my son's name. I was scared that my son might have been upstairs in the bedroom and that the gunman had gone after him.

When Mrs Saville saw me talking to the so-called killer I was actually speaking to the man unloading his shopping before he ran off to fetch the policeman from the park.

In fact, a team of detectives led by Detective Superintendent Mick Morgan had conducted a painstaking inquiry which resulted in the comprehensive case being made out against Calvey and Reece.

Post-mortem reports showed that Cook had indeed been shot twice. The first shot had hit him near the elbow, causing little damage, but the second shot had been right on target. According to the pathologist, the gun had been angled above Cook's head when the trigger was pulled.

In Linda's kitchen were a set of at first unidentified fingerprints, but a search of the National Fingerprint Collection soon revealed that they belonged to Reece, a man the police had no reason to connect with Mrs Calvey up to that point. Inquiries quickly established that he had been on prison leave the day of the killing. The clothes he had worn were taken for scientific examination and on his jacket, a present from Calvey, was the unmistakable residue left by a gun being fired.

During the trial the prosecution made much of the fact that independent witnesses had seen Danny Reece loitering in the park before the shooting and others could testify that he caught a train back to his prison in Dorset that same afternoon. Why, asked prosecuting counsel, had Linda Calvey studiously avoided mentioning the fact that Danny Reece was out of prison and spending the weekend with her?

The defence, led by the eminent QC Ronald Thwaites, laid out Linda's version of events in great detail. Her story obviously held great sway with at least one member of the jury, which deliberated for two days: Calvey and Reece were both found guilty of Cook's murder by a verdict of eleven to one.

Passing a sentence of life imprisonment the judge Mr Justice Hidden said: 'This crime was carried out in cold blood and in ruthless circumstances. There is only one penalty.'

Linda recalls:

The trial lasted about four-and-a-half weeks but it seemed like six months. The jury were out for two full days. The judge asked for a unanimous verdict at the end of the first day but they couldn't agree. So just about an hour before the end of the second day he called them back into court and urged them to reach a majority verdict.

They came back forty-five minutes later and brought in a majority guilty verdict. It was the wrong verdict.

To this day I still wonder whether that jury ever think back and worry about what they did to us. Do they ever wonder whether they were right or wrong? All these years later I still can't believe that I am sitting in prison with a life sentence.

2

HALL OF INFAMY

When the foreman of the jury said: 'Guilty, your honour', I was stunned.

I felt as if I'd been punched in the face by Mike Tyson. I hadn't thought for a minute, not for a single moment, that they would find me guilty. When the judge sentenced me to life imprisonment it was as if I'd gone to see the doctor with a cold and been told that I only had weeks to live. The horror and disbelief knocked me for six.

I looked at Danny. There was a single tear trickling down his cheek. 'I'm crying for you, not me,' he whispered.

I held his hand tight as we were led down to the cells. At the bottom of the stairs he hugged me and said: 'We will never give up. We will prove our innocence.'

They took him off one way and me another. The next day the

newspaper headlines read: 'The Black Widow showed no emotion when she was given life.'

No emotion? What did they know? Inside I was dying.

Much of Linda's time at the Old Bailey had been spent waiting in the main female holding suite in the basement, deep below the courts. It is a sad and lonely place. The walls are covered with graffiti spelling out messages of defiance, despair, and the inevitable quota of cheeky gallows humour which is the prisoners' age-old safety valve against the pressure of their predicament. Linda goes on:

One of my unfortunate predecessors had used a felt-tipped pen to draw an elaborate archway around the door, and had written above it in large bold lettering 'The Hall of Fame'. When I spotted that I said to myself: 'I think you mean The Hall of Infamy, don't you?'

After my conviction it was here that I sat and pondered my fate as I waited to be called back for the judge to pass sentence. The graffiti on the walls spoke powerfully to me. Barely a square inch had not been written on with the names of dozens of strangers alongside their sentences. Ominously most of them starkly bore the single word 'Life'.

One group stood out. Six very young men had tried to cheer themselves up by penning saucy poems. One of their number had been acquitted. His name bore the inscription 'Lucky Bastard'. The others had all got sentences of around twenty years and I thought to myself: 'How sad. They probably weren't bad. They just did it like everyone else to try and get a better standard of living.'

As she sat staring at the graffiti on the cell walls Linda began to reflect on her life and the marriage to Michael Calvey which was to set in train the chain of events which had brought her to this fateful day:

* * *

Our marriage was full of ups and downs. Micky was always out on some blag or another and I got used to him being put away. He'd been in prison quite a bit before we met and he got nicked a couple more times after we were married. By December 1978 we had been married for nearly ten years and he'd been inside for much of that time.

Micky never actually told me he was doing a robbery but I knew that when he said he was out 'working' that's what he meant. It was an unspoken rule between us – he didn't tell me and I didn't ask.

But the job he took that December was very different . . .

My Micky always went out for a drink on a Friday night, staying out 'til late. On this particular Friday night he came home early and told me he was doing a bit of 'work' the next Saturday.

He'd been in prison from the age of twenty-one to twenty-eight, so he had never learned to drive. It didn't bother him. He liked being picked up and driven about. I think it gave him a sense of importance – a little bit of luxury. Whenever he was on a bit of 'work' he was always picked up.

All the robbery firms liked working with Micky because, as he didn't drive, he used to compensate by being the anchorman. That meant he would go in and hold the fort while everyone else did the job, got clear and came out. He was really staunch because anchorman was the position nobody wanted. Being the last one out was really risky and you needed a cool nerve to hold guards, staff and the public at bay while alarms were ringing and you could probably hear the sound of police car sirens approaching in the distance.

On the Saturday morning he was getting ready to go on the job. He came downstairs and told me he was off. 'I'll be home about six,' he said.

I thought it was a bit strange that nobody was coming to pick him up but he just brushed it off by saying he was working with different people. I carried on with my normal day, getting the kids ready and doing a bit of shopping – nothing very exciting. Then I got dinner ready.

When he came in he had a long face. 'No need to ask,' I said. 'No,' he said. 'We missed it. We're gutted.'

The timing of cash robberies is crucial. The robbers must not break cover before the money has been released from the strongroom into the care of the security guards. The best opportunity to snatch it at gunpoint is as the cashboxes or bags are being carried across the pavement to the armoured van. Move too soon and security staff might have the chance to retreat back into the safety of the building. Move too late and the prize will be locked away in the safe of the armoured van. Everything must be done in a matter of seconds – arrive, hold up the guards, and get away.

On this occasion, Micky said, the gang had only just missed the money by a couple of minutes and he was furious. 'It's nearly Christmas. I've got to have it. I'm going again next week,' he vowed. I knew he didn't like going back to something, but he said he was relying on the money for Christmas and he didn't have anything else in the pipeline.

All week he moped around the house. Come Saturday the same thing happened: he got ready and off he went. I thought to myself: 'I hope he gets it today, the miserable sod.'

I pottered around all day and then got the dinner ready as usual. At 6.30 I heard the door slam. He didn't even speak. He went straight upstairs and when I heard him running a bath I knew I'd better leave him alone.

Eventually he came down with a face so long he could have tucked it into his underpants. I asked him what the matter was and he just snapped: 'We missed it again!'

I said, 'Perhaps you ain't meant to have it then.'

He got really annoyed at that. 'Never mind, I ain't meant to have it. I've got to have it,' he yelled.

He was going on about how he'd got to get the kids presents for Christmas and how he wasn't going to let it go. He was going again next week. I looked him straight in the eye and said 'You don't want to go, do you?'

I could sense the answer so I wasn't surprised when he replied: 'No, I truly, truly don't want to go. It's a bad bit of work. I've been twice already. It's an omen . . . but I've got nothing else.'

It was at that moment that I had an awful premonition. I began to plead with him not to go on the job. I said I would ask my mum and dad for a temporary loan. I was sure they would lend us a couple of hundred pounds just to tide us over Christmas, but he wouldn't hear of it. He wouldn't ponce off my parents, he said. It wasn't on.

I was so nervous and so insistent that Micky said he would ask around during the week to see if he could raise the cash we needed. A couple of friends owed him money and he promised that if he got that back he would give the job a miss.

He asked various people but he had no joy. By mid-week he said he was in a corner. He had no choice. He had to go. I was furious that he'd got knock-backs from people who owed him because everybody knew that whenever Micky was flush he would always help people out. However, that was his business and I could do nothing but keep out of it.

On the Thursday he got his Giro cheque and said: 'Come on, I'm going to buy you something for Christmas.' We took the kids round to my mum's and set off for the market. Micky said he wanted to buy me a dress.

We had a standing joke that his favourite colour was lavender. I always kidded him that he would fancy me in a coal sack as long as it was lavender.

That day we spotted in a shop window a plain dress with boot-lace straps and a lavender lace bolero. He loved it and made me go in and try it on. While I was in the changing cubicle the assistant told him that it also came in black. When I came out with the lavender dress on he said it looked blinding but he wanted me to try on the black one too. I laughed my head off. 'That's a waste of time,' I giggled, 'you know your favourite colour is lavender.' But strangely enough, for the first time ever, he chose the black instead of the lavender.

'It looks great, Sweetheart! Wear it when we go out on Saturday night,' he smiled. 'If I crack it Saturday, I'll buy you the lavender one as well.'

When we came out of the shop Micky insisted that I go back and pick up the kids. He wanted to buy them a few bits for Christmas. I thought he'd run out of money, but he told me just to go home and he'd be back later. So I collected the kids from my mum. After a couple of hours he came home and I couldn't believe my eyes. He had all the Christmas trimmings.

'Where on earth did you get all that?' I asked in amazement.

He didn't want to tell me at first, but in the end he said that one of his friends had given him a stolen chequebook with a counterfeit bank card and shown him how to use it. This particular scam is known as 'kiting' in the underworld. Micky had never done kiting before – it wasn't his bag – but at least, he said, he knew the kids would have a decent Christmas.

He had bought Melanie an old-fashioned doll's pram with big iron wheels and a wickerwork body. It was lovely. She still has it. Neil got a desk and a chair, and there were lots of bits and pieces for under the tree and all the decorations.

I had been working at various markets a couple of days a week and that Friday I was helping my mum on a knitting wool stall down in Maidstone. When I got home Micky and the kids met me at the front door.

'Tell Mummy to close her eyes,' he said. Then as I walked in he added with more than a hint of pride: 'Open them. Me and the kids did this for you.'

They had decorated the hallway and the front room. Micky had used the stolen cheques to buy the decorations so there were absolutely bundles of them. There was an artificial tree all decorated with fairy lights. It was such a lovely surprise. Everything looked so pretty – like Santa's grotto.

You can imagine the state my kids were in. They were over the moon that they had spent all day doing this with their dad. Melanie was eight at the time and Neil was only four. In the years to come I was so glad that they had this last enduring happy memory of their father.

On the sideboard were two piles of Christmas cards. Micky told me that he had written them all out. One pile was for the family and the other for all his mates inside. All I had to do, he said, was to stick on the stamps and post them.

We had our dinner and put the kids to bed. Later in the evening, when we sat together holding hands, things seemed so peaceful. I felt contented. We had the children's toys and all the decorations for Christmas. I leant over and whispered in Micky's ear. 'Leave it now. Don't go back on that job tomorrow.'

He just looked at me for a long time and then said very gently: 'No, Darling, I can't. I have to go.'

The next day he came running downstairs calling: 'I'm off,' as he let himself out. A couple of minutes later he was back. He'd forgotten his gloves. He banged on the front door and said: 'Look, I ain't coming in. It's pissing hard. I don't want to take my boots off. Just nip up to the bathroom for me, will you love? I forgot my gloves.'

While I was fetching the gloves little Melanie peeped out and said: 'Daddy, come in you're getting wet.'

I ran down the stairs, handed Micky the gloves and said: 'Go on then, you don't want to be late.' I gave him a quick peck on the cheek and shut the front door.

All my Melanie had seen was her dad standing in the doorway and later, for weeks afterwards, every time she saw me she screamed: 'You killed my daddy! You did! You wouldn't let him in.'

I'm still slaughtered by the memory of that. Little children are so vulnerable and trusting. Just when I was hurting so desperately I had to cope with the thought that my little eight-year-old daughter hated me and blamed me for the loss of her father.

At the age of thirty-seven Michael Calvey was already a hardened criminal – a man coolly skilled in the black art of armed robbery at the point of a sawn-off shotgun. In 1963, when he was just twenty-two years old, an Old Bailey judge gave him eight years for his part in robbing four Marks and Spencer's employees of cash. When he and Linda married in 1970 he was doing time for a £52,000 robbery, and in 1976 he had been jailed for two years after being exposed by the supergrass Charlie Lowe.

As he left the house that chill December Saturday, however, Calvey could not have imagined how tragically prescient his feelings of foreboding would prove to be. He was walking straight into a trap.

In the previous twelve months there had been twenty-two violent armed robberies in that part of south-east London and there was genuine public anger over the fact that the villains seemed to be flouting the law with apparent impunity. Stung by this criticism, Scotland Yard chiefs were determined to put a stop to the spate of cash thefts and the Flying Squad had been tasked to mount an undercover operation.

The repeated postponement of the Calvey gang's intended robbery allowed news of the plan to seep out into the twilight world of police informers and soon the Yard knew the day and the time of the heist but, crucially, not the precise target. The idea was to hit a large supermarket just after the tills had been cashed up at the end of a busy pre-Christmas Saturday. However, there were dozens of suitable targets in the region and the problem for detectives was to pick the right one. The only solution seemed to be to send out teams of armed officers to cruise the streets in the hope of spotting known criminals lying in wait.

So it was that Detective Sergeant Michael Banks and Michael Calvey came to meet.

Banks, and his two colleagues, Detective Constables Stuart Gillies and Thomas Carwyn, chose to park their unmarked police car outside Caters Supermarket in Eltham High Street. It was 5 p.m. – just before closing time. Only Banks was armed with a regulation issue .38 Smith and Wesson revolver.

The pavements were thronged with shoppers as a Securicor van drew up and guards began to load the days takings of £10,000 on board. Suddenly a white Rover car, with its headlights flashing and horn blaring, hurtled past and skidded to a halt in front of the van. Three armed men tumbled out. One of the robbers, Calvey, was wearing a white coat and began beating one of the security guards over the head with the butt of a double-barrelled shotgun.

Banks had only rehearsed such a scene at police training school so he automatically did as his instructors had told him. 'Stop! Armed police!' he bellowed.

One of the robbers dived into the front seat of the getaway car with a sawn-off shotgun across his lap. As shoppers screamed and scattered, Banks again yelled: 'We are armed police! Drop your guns!' The robber simply raised his shotgun and pointed it at the detective. Fearing that he might accidentally hit a member of the public, Banks fired low – at the man's legs. The car door slammed shut and the driver gunned the engine as, with a squeal of tyres, the vehicle began to move.

Then it was that the policemen spotted Calvey. He was running, crouched crab-like alongside the car, trying to get into the rear door. According to evidence given later at the inquest, the shotgun was in Calvey's right hand as he tried to open the door with his left.

Banks screamed his order to drop the gun again, but, unlike the scenarios he had practised in training, the robber abandoned the getaway car and, crouching in the middle of the road, he grabbed his gun in both hands and aimed straight at Banks's midriff.

Banks fired twice and Calvey fell dead in the roadway.

Meanwhile his young wife, Linda, was going about her domestic chores, unaware of the drama unfolding just a few miles away on the other side of the Thames:

The day that was to change my life forever was unremarkably routine.

As we were planning to go out in the evening, I dropped the kids off at my mum's, got a bit of shopping in, and cooked a lovely roast chicken dinner. By 5.30 I was thinking to myself: 'He'll be home in a minute.'

Six o'clock came and went.

I thought: 'Sod him. I'll eat my dinner.' I turned the oven down, put a plate over his food so it wouldn't dry up, and began to prepare for the evening. By the time I was ready he would be home, I reckoned. I ran a bath, put my heated rollers in my hair, and laid my new black dress out on the bed.

I smiled to myself as I soaked in the bath. 'I know what's happened,' I thought. 'He's cracked it. He's got the money and he's so relieved he's gone for a drink and got a little bit involved.'

I put on my dressing gown and made myself a cup of coffee. By this time it was getting on for 7.30 and I was just about to switch on the telly when there was a knock at the door. It was Jerry and his girlfriend, the friends we were going out with. They were early.

Jerry must have seen the concerned look on my face because he asked straight away: 'Where is he? Is he all right?'

I told him Micky wasn't home. He looked puzzled. 'What do you mean, he ain't home yet? I don't like the sound of this,' he said. He knew Micky had gone on a job but, like me, he had no idea who he was with.

I was starting to worry. I suggested to Jerry that maybe they'd cracked it and Micky had gone for a drink to celebrate. 'Yeah, yeah, that's it, Babe,' he said comfortingly, but I knew that he was only humouring me.

There were only four pubs he'd be likely to go to, so we decided to look for him. I ran upstairs and put on my new dress. It's ironic that the night Micky died I was in black because it was a colour I hardly ever wore.

We left the house just before the eight o'clock news. A few minutes later and we would have seen that there had been an armed robbery in Eltham and one of the robbers had been shot dead. Of course I didn't know where the robbery was to be, but I think I would have put two and two together.

In the event I missed the news and, apparently, twenty minutes after I went out the police arrived at our house to inform me. I missed them too. I bet they were relieved I wasn't home. They went to Micky's mum's, but she's deaf and didn't hear them so, eventually, they broke the tragic news to his brother. He promised to let me know.

Still oblivious to the dramatic events which were about to engulf us, Jerry, his girlfriend and I set off for Micky's favourite pub, The Needlegun, down the Roman Road. At the time it was run by friends of ours, so I went straight up to the bar and asked: 'Has my Micky been in?'

'No, Darling, I ain't seen him,' replied the landlady.

I asked her to let him know I was looking for him if he came in later, and to tell him that I was going to another of his favourite haunts, The Carpenters.

We went to The Carpenters. He wasn't there.

In the end we did the rounds but Micky was nowhere to be found. We finished up in a pub in Hackney owned by other friends of ours called Ron and Sylvie.

I rushed in and breathlessly asked Sylvie if Micky had been in. She smiled reassuringly and said that he'd telephoned with a message for me to stay there and he would be back later.

In fact, Micky had told Sylvie the night before that he was doing a job and, having seen the television news, she guessed that it was Micky who had been shot. However, she wasn't sure and, later, she told me that all she could think of saying when I came in looking for Micky was that he'd phoned, just to keep me in the pub with friends.

At the time, of course, I didn't know any of this.

By about 2 a.m. I had the right hump. Micky still hadn't turned up, so I decided to go home.

I thought it was a bit strange when I saw Sylvie take Jerry to one side and whisper something to him. The next minute they were all saying that they'd come back with me.

'No, Micky will probably be home when I get there,' I insisted, but they were having none of it. Sylvie was quite firm, she was coming with me.

When we pulled up in a cab, the house was still in darkness. I was baffled.

By this time it had turned 3 a.m. 'You just wait 'til he gets home!' I moaned to Sylvie as she made us a cup of coffee, but she simply said: 'Come on darling, go to bed, get some sleep,' with an unnaturally comforting edge to her voice which I didn't recognise until I looked back on that night months later.

I got into bed. I wasn't worried any more because Sylvie had said Micky had phoned. I was just angry that he still hadn't come home.

The next thing I knew the phone was ringing. It was Micky's brother Terry. Still a bit bleary-eyed I greeted him with: 'Hello Terry, bit early for you to ring ain't it? What's up?'

He stuttered a bit and then said: 'Look, I've had the Old Bill on. Micky's been nicked. You'd better come over here now.'

When I told him Sylvie was with me, he simply said: 'Good. Get a cab.'

I called out to Sylvie: 'Sylv, he's been nicked. We've got to go to his brother's.'

I ran around frantically getting ready, picking up a few things that I thought my Micky would need. Sylvie took the bag out of my hand and reassuringly said: 'He won't need anything, Darling. Terry will have sorted that.'

'Yeah, you're right,' I said.

We got a cab to Brabazon Street, Poplar. Terry lived in a tall block of flats and while we took the lift I was chatting away to Sylv. She wasn't saying much.

The design of Terry's flat was typical of most homes in the East End tower blocks built during the sixties – as you open the street door there's a weenie passage, then it runs into a long passage with all the doors off into the bedrooms and lounge. I reached the front door where Terry was waiting for me. It must have been hard for him. First to phone me with some cock-and-bull story to get me there and then, when he'd got me there, he had to tell me.

I breezed in and cheerily asked: 'Well, where is he Tel? What's happened?'

Suddenly something odd began to dawn on me. A question flashed across my mind: 'What are all these people doing in Terry's flat at this time on a Sunday morning?'

My mum was there. 'Hello Mum, what are you doing here?' I asked. There was an awkward silence. What was she doing there? It was weird. They were all looking at me. I said: 'What's going on?'

Terry put his arm around me. Very gently he simply said: 'Micky's dead, Lin.'

At that moment everything in me went blank and cold. I was totally numb. All I can remember is hearing someone screaming and screaming. I was thinking: 'Who's that screaming? Make them shut up.' But it was me.

Someone shouted: 'Slap her round the face. She's hysterical.'

I don't know if anyone did hit me or not. All I can remember is Terry's wife giving me a brandy saying, 'Drink this, Darling.'

Slowly Terry told me what had happened – that the police said that Micky had been on an armed robbery and had come face to face with a copper. Micky is supposed to have said: 'It's me or you copper,' and there had been a shoot-out. The police said they had no choice but to shoot Micky through the stomach and he died.

I screamed at Terry, 'No, Micky wouldn't do that!'

Terry tried to comfort me. He said: 'It's got to be right, Lin. The Old Bill have told me.'

I didn't know what to do. I asked Terry what happened next. He said as I was Micky's wife I had to go and identify his body. We drove over to south London. There was a heavy frost that morning and I was freezing cold, but nothing was as cold as the chill I felt as I went into that morgue. I felt like I was watching someone else do all these things.

As I walked in I was met by a policeman holding a piece of paper for me to sign. It was odd. He hardly gave me time to get in the door before he thrust the paper in my hand and snapped: 'Sign here.'

I just looked at him and said: 'Where's my Micky?'

I wasn't going to sign any bits of paper until I knew exactly what had happened. The policeman took me towards a small window and told me to look through it. A big fat man in a white coat wheeled out a trolley with a white sheet over it. As he approached the window he pulled back the cover. It was my Micky. I started to cry. So did Terry.

The policeman asked: 'Is this your husband?'

Quietly, I answered: 'Yes.'

'Sign here,' the policeman said again and tapped the pen on his clipboard. I snatched the board out of his hand and threw it on the floor. There was my Micky lying dead on that trolley and all he was interested in was a stupid piece of paper.

I knew there was something funny about the whole thing by the way the police were acting. They would only let me see my husband's face from behind the glass. I know that is routine but I still had a feeling of deep disquiet inside me. One thing was certain in my mind, Micky would never have threatened to have a shoot-out with the police. I knew my husband so I knew in my heart that he would not have done that.

I was in bits. One day I had a husband, the next day he was gone. I knew I had to prove the truth or Micky would never be at rest.

The policeman's attitude changed when I said that they were lying about how my husband died and I wouldn't accept it. He tried to reason with Terry who said: 'Look love, just sign his piece of paper and let us get our Micky out of here.'

I was adamant, however, and from that day on the police and I have had no love for each other. Any respect I had for them before then, and believe it or not I did respect the police, died along with Micky. I am sorry that I feel like this. I am sure that the decent coppers must outnumber the ones that I have encountered along the way, but I am afraid that there is more corruption, bullying and racial discrimination in the name of the law than the British public deserve.

At the time I was too distressed to be able to put my finger on what was wrong, but I was determined to get to the bottom of my Micky's death. As soon as I got home I phoned my solicitor and, with his help, we put up a big fight with the police. They said my Micky was shot in the stomach but I didn't believe them. I told them I wanted an independent post-mortem and my post-mortem clearly stated that Micky was shot in the back.

What was going on?

This dispute over how Calvey came to be killed rumbled on for many months. The police insisted that the detective was being directly threatened and fired to protect himself, his colleagues and the public. Calvey's family were insistent that Micky was threatening no one, simply trying to get away, and was shot in the back as he retreated.

When it came to the inquest, their claims seemed to be supported by the Home Office pathologist Professor James Cameron, who agreed that the fatal bullet had entered the dead man's back between the bottom two ribs – just above and to the left of the base of the spine – travelling right through the body and out at the front at a 30-degree angle. Under cross-examination, however, the pathologist demonstrated that Calvey had been half-turned at the time he was hit and could, as the witnesses insisted, have been pointing a gun at the pursuing police officers.

In fact, the coroner told the police officers that their action was justified and should be commended.

'If I had not fired I would have been cut to pieces,' Detective Sergeant Banks told coroner Arthur Gordon-Davies at Southwark Coroner's court. Twice he had faced death by shotgun when he intervened in the raid. He had fired twice low into the getaway car at an armed man threatening him with a sawn-off shotgun. Then he had fired twice more at a second gunman swinging round to face him – and this time Michael Calvey fell dying.

'I believe that if I had not fired I would be dead,' Banks told the inquest. 'I thought I was dead on two occasions.'

Mr Gordon-Davies told the jury: 'A sawn-off shotgun is a horrible weapon. If it had been fired, many people could have been killed. The officer himself would have been cut in half and the security guards badly injured. The law of this country says that the action taken by Sergeant Banks was not only justifiable homicide but he should be greatly commended for his courage.'

All of this, of course, was of little comfort to Linda Calvey as she struggled to deal with the media attention and the smothering support being offered by the underworld fraternity. Linda recalled:

Afterwards we took Micky home. We wanted him home for the last time so we could say goodbye to him properly. The funeral directors came and laid my Micky out in his coffin in the front room. They told us to turn off all the heating and, during the day, to open the windows. It was very noisy because the council were digging up the road outside and the constant drilling and banging were driving us mad.

Throughout the next couple of days the house seemed full of people – all sorts, and some I'd never even met before. They all wanted to pay their respects. All the family was there too and Maureen, Micky's sister, decided to stay overnight with me. With all the windows open the house was freezing cold, but Micky's mum came to the rescue and brought us a couple of her nightdresses, the old-fashioned ones made out of white wincyette, which came right down to the ground.

That first night Maureen and I huddled together to keep warm. I closed my eyes and started to drift off when, all of a sudden, I heard a voice call out 'Help!'

I sat up and listened. I was sure I must be dreaming. Then I heard it again: 'Help!'

I shook Maureen. 'Wake up, wake up,' I yelled. 'Micky's not dead, he's calling me.'

All bleary-eyed she kissed me on the forehead and said: 'Bless your heart, Darling, you're dreaming, go back to sleep.'

'Yeah, you're right, I must have been dreaming,' I said. But as soon as I put my head on the pillow I heard it again: 'Help!'

This time Maureen heard it too. She sat bolt upright and said: 'Blimey, you're right.'

We grabbed each other by the hand and started to make our way downstairs. We were scared stiff and when we got outside the front room door we started to argue about who was going in first.

'He's your brother,' I said.

'Yeah, but he's your husband,' she replied.

We crept in quietly and peered into the coffin. Micky was still in there and he was dead all right. Then again we heard: 'Help!'

'Someone's having a game with us,' said Maureen, cursing under her breath as she ran outside, but she couldn't see anyone.

'Help!' it came again.

Maureen went outside the front gate to the big hole that the workmen had been digging. She looked over the edge to see a drunken man shouting 'Help!' When he saw her, he screamed his head off and scrambled out unaided.

The next day the man's wife came over and apologised. She said: 'I'm sorry. All he saw was this figure above him, peering at him, dressed in a long white robe. He thought you were a ghost.'

My Micky was shot on 9 December 1978, but I wasn't allowed to bury him until 8 January 1979. His funeral made the front page of all the newspapers and over 200 mourners came to show their respects. Everyone liked my Micky.

In February I went to the coroner's inquest and heard the jury's verdict: justifiable homicide.

Detective Sergeant Banks, the officer who had shot him, even received a commendation. I couldn't believe it. What a liberty! I couldn't hold back my anger any longer. I walked up to him, and shouted: 'Show my kids the commendation you got for killing their father!'

It wasn't right that he should be allowed to get away with killing my Micky then say all those things.

By this time I was exhausted. All that had happened affected me badly. I became bitter and nothing seemed to matter any more. Part of me died when I buried my Micky. And so did my respect for the police and the authorities.

The Coroner's Court outburst was the moment which was to earn Linda Calvey her Black Widow nickname. All the newspapers reported that she had screamed 'Bastard!' at Sergeant Banks and had added: 'I would like to introduce you to my children as the man who murdered their father.'

A few newspapers revealed that Banks turned away and quietly said to colleagues: 'It could have been my wife without a husband and my two children without a father today.'

Linda's loyalty to her husband's memory was unwavering. She told the *News of the World*:

> The telephone hasn't stopped ringing with offers of help and sympathy. People have been asking if they can come to the funeral and pay their respects. And it's not from villains and criminals either. Pubs have been holding raffles to raise money to pay the solicitor.
>
> How can Micky have been such a bad man as the police have made him out and still get all this support?
>
> They quickly published details of his past after the shooting. They said he was sentenced to eight years in 1963 for robbery. They said he was violent.
>
> What they didn't say was that he was recognised in that raid when he went back to stop someone with him from beating one of the victims.
>
> During that trial an ex-mayor of Tower Hamlets went to tell the court that Micky used to help him with charity work in boys' clubs.
>
> To get a town's leading citizen to do that must show that he wasn't as bad as everyone is making out.

Overnight Linda had become a public figure and the public were divided in their attitude to her predicament. The *Sunday Mirror* newspaper summed it up neatly in a leader column which read:

> It is not difficult to sympathise with Mrs Linda Calvey who shouted 'Murderer!' and 'Bastard!' at the police officer who killed her husband.
>
> Not difficult to sympathise because she loved Michael

Calvey, even though he was a criminal, and because she loves her two children who are now fatherless.

But how can anyone sympathise with Calvey himself? He was a violent, brutish thug who brought terror to the streets and had a record as long as your arm.

It was an incredibly brave act of Detective Sergeant Banks, armed with a revolver, to leave his patrol car and confront three robbers with powerful sawn-off shotguns.

Last week's Southwark inquest heard how Banks, seeing one of the robbers club down a security guard outside a London supermarket, shouted a warning to them to drop their guns.

He told the court that he fired when Calvey half-turned in a crouching position and pointed his gun.

The pathologist said that Calvey had been shot in the back, but it was perfectly possible for him to have been sideways-on, pointing the gun when he was hit.

The dead man's gun was later found to be loaded in both barrels, ready to fire.

So who would care to question the policeman's belief that he would have been 'cut to pieces' if he had not fired at the robber?

Kindly folk can sympathise with Mrs Calvey and her children. But there is no doubt who was the 'bastard' in this case. Her husband.

3

THE EASTENDER

The cockneys of London's East End are known worldwide for their sense of humour and their down-to-earth approach to life. The history of the Second World War is punctuated with stories of immense bravery and appalling suffering endured during the Blitz and beyond by the most close-knit of communities in Britain's capital city.

Linda's upbringing at the heart of this vibrant and energetic community was typical of her post-war generation – large families cheerily staring adversity in the face and making ends meet by hard work and a willingness to share what little they had with their neighbours. As she tells it, her childhood and teenage years certainly gave little clue to the extraordinary path her adult life would take:

I am the daughter of a blacksmith. To this day, even at eighty years of age, my father Charlie Welford is still working as a blacksmith – the only one in the East End of London. It is a family business going back several generations. He was the youngest of seven children and the only one to keep the business going all these years.

My mother Eileen is the eldest of three sisters from a family which owned a dairy and ran a café. So, although they both grew up in the East End, neither of my parents came from a poor background. They are both honest, hardworking, decent people. They cannot, in their wildest dreams, or should I say nightmares, have imagined what was to happen to me.

I am one of nine children – three boys and six girls. I am second in line and the eldest girl. My older brother, Terry, is three years my senior. He and I were both born in a private nursing home in Ilford, Essex. The other seven were all born in National Health hospitals and when we were young Terry and I used to tease the others that Mum and Dad paid for us but got them free.

When I was five years old the family moved to a new post-war housing estate in Stepney to be near my dad's blacksmith firm. We had a four-bedroomed ground-floor maisonette in Welton House, Stepney Way where we all grew up. It was quite cramped with eleven people living on top of one another, but I have lovely memories of my childhood and teenage years. With so many kids to look after my mother was a full-time mum, so we only had my father's income to live off, but, even though there was very little money to go round, we could not have wished for better parents. Our house was full of love.

I can honestly say that my dad never raised a hand to any of us or to my mum. He would have a moan from time to time, but he was really easygoing and would never dream of ever upsetting any of us.

My mother was the central figure. She was the head and in total charge of all aspects of family life. My dad favoured the girls and my mum favoured the boys, so we all knew which one of our parents we could get around easiest.

Even though money was tight, we each got a new coat, a new pair of shoes and a new outfit every Christmas. At Easter every year all the girls got new shoes and a dress and the boys got new trousers and a shirt. For the rest of the year my mum would go to the Mission shop or jumble sales for clothes.

As a family we always ate well. My father's job was very physically demanding, so he came home every lunchtime for a full cooked meal and in the evening would again eat a hearty dinner. He did a lot of work in both the fish and the meat markets and many of his customers would pay him in kind, so there was always plenty of fresh food in our house. I remember also there was a huge tea chest full of tea kept under the stairs.

Both my parents are staunch royalists and members of the Conservative party. I was brought up to be the same. Even to this day I am proud to say that I love the royal family and support the Conservatives. At the time when the trade unions were so powerful in Britain, virtually running the country, my father's strong anti-union views used to make us kids smile. All the dockers had to come and have their dockers' hooks made by my dad and he never missed an opportunity to give them his political opinions. Perhaps that is where I get my outspokenness from.

My early life was very uneventful. Most of our time was spent playing in the bombsites which were dotted all over the East End just after the war. Every summer we went for a two-week caravan holiday, either to Great Yarmouth or sometimes to Devon.

I began my schooling at the same school my mother had attended, Marion Richardson Primary and Junior School in Senrab Street. Unlike most of my brothers and sisters, I was a bit of a dunce at schoolwork. My brother Tony and I went on to Dempsey Street secondary modern school and we both left with no academic qualifications.

My sister Shelley was our real brainbox, but I guess Terry has done the best of all. He is a self-made millionaire and master of his Masonic lodge. He is also one of the kindest and nicest-natured people you could find. I feel very proud of him.

Mind you, all my brothers and sisters have done quite well. That would be the influence of my mother. She brought us up to believe that nobody was better than us and gave us the confidence to achieve anything we set our minds to. She gave us ambition and taught us that nothing was impossible if we believed in ourselves. She also taught us to be kind and have good manners. I guess all that any of us has achieved is due to her belief in us.

When I was about eleven my father and my uncle Jim bought some concrete bases on a caravan park called Bell Farm at Minster on the Isle of Sheppey. They used the bases to build a number of holiday chalets to rent out and kept a chalet each for the use of their own families. Our chalet was called Sky High and for years after that we spent all our school holidays down there, and as many weekends as we could get away. We loved going to the clubhouse to buy crisps and lemonade and join in the community singalongs. It was a brilliant atmosphere.

Years later I returned to check on our chalet. All the caravans were still on the site but, to my great sorrow, all that was left of the chalets was the original concrete bases. They had been made of asbestos and so had to be torn down for health reasons. It was almost as if they had never been there, as if my happy childhood times had been only dreams.

I am very fond of all my in-laws but I am particularly close to my sister Maxine's husband Peter. He lives in Marbella in Spain and Maxine spends most of her time travelling between London and the Costa del Sol. Whenever they visit, they insist that I should go and live there. I must say that I am tempted. Much as I love England, I think I should look for a second home abroad.

I am constantly amazed by the part that fate plays in our lives –

certainly in mine – but you don't come to realise it until something traumatic happens like losing the one you love forever. Then you look back and everything is clear. I can see now that, in a way, it is through my Micky that I am where I am today.

I first met Micky in 1969.

At the time I was involved with a married man called Terry and had been seeing him for something like four years. I had never had a boyfriend while I was growing up and had never even given boys a second thought. I was only young, sweet sixteen, when the affair with him started and before I knew it, there I was, aged twenty-four, years into a relationship that was going nowhere, and it was starting to get to me. All the things that Mum and Dad had warned me about were coming true. They were right. It was no good. In the years we had been together I had never met any of his family – or anyone he knew, come to that. I was just his little secret.

I was young and I was getting pretty fed up with his broken promises. It was the same old familiar story. Him telling me that he loved me and that he would tell his wife, but the time wasn't right. 'Just give me time,' he used to say. I wonder how many mistresses have heard that before?

In those days I was working as a receptionist at Smithson's paint factory in Whitechapel Road, opposite The Blind Beggar pub. It wasn't much of a job, but it was handy because I lived just around the corner in Stepney Way.

All I ever seemed to do was quarrel with Terry. Things came to a head one Thursday evening. I screamed at him that nothing had changed in the four years I'd been with him, I was still in the same position as Day One, and I didn't want to see him over the weekend. I needed time to think.

The next day I was miserable, but as it was Friday I got my wages and decided to cheer myself up with a new dress. I had seen this right nice little number earlier in the week in a market down the road. It was a bright pink mini-dress with a big spotted bow on the front. It sounds grotesque now, but at the time I thought it was absolutely beautiful.

I packed up my things early, got my money and set off. As I was strolling through the market, looking at all the stalls, I bumped into my cousin Patsy and her husband George. He took one look at me and said: 'What's the matter with you, Babe? You seem right pissed off.'

'Yeah, I am. I've just come down here to cheer myself up by buying a new dress.' I told them all about the row I'd had with Terry, how he still hadn't left his wife, and how I wasn't seeing him over the weekend.

Suddenly George became animated. 'Hang on a minute,' he said, 'if you ain't seeing him 'til Monday, you ain't doing anything this weekend, are ya?'

I said: 'I suppose not.'

'Well you are now,' he said. 'One of my friends has just come out of prison after doing an eight stretch for robbing a Marks and Spencer's security van – we're having a party for him.'

I was very reluctant but George explained that everyone going to the party would have a partner and his friend would feel awkward without a woman to escort: 'Me and Patsy have been trying to think of someone halfway decent to go to the party with him. He's right nice. You'll like him.'

That was enough to convince me that my date was bound to be rough. I had never met anyone who had been in prison before so I assumed that he would have an IQ of minus ten, a broken nose, and look like a robber's dog.

George giggled and assured me that his friend did not have a broken nose. 'Come on, you're only twenty, you don't want to sit in on a Saturday night!' he urged. 'Look, you've got your new dress to wear.'

So, eventually, I agreed. I wonder how my life would have turned out if I'd refused.

The next day I made a half-hearted effort to get ready. I put my long blonde hair in rollers, put on my false eyelashes and make-up, and laid my new pink mini-dress on the bed, but my heart wasn't in it. I put on my dressing gown and slumped in front of the telly, telling my mum that I was missing Terry and didn't want to go partying.

I wasn't going to get out of it that easily. The telephone rang and it was Patsy. 'Lin, are you ready?' she asked. 'The bloke's feeling a mug waiting for you. Every time the door opens he looks up and says "Is that her?" Now don't mug us off. Get your dress on and come down. I've phoned a cab. It's on its way.'

So, dressed the part in the pink dress and a pink and green hounds-tooth jacket, I set off with more than a little trepidation.

When I walked into the pub, The Blue Anchor, the first thing I saw was George standing at the bar with a really tasty-looking man. 'Well obviously that can't be him,' I thought to myself. 'He's far too nice.'

Patsy grabbed me by the arm and dragged me over. George winked at me. 'Linda, this is Micky. Micky, this is Linda,' he said as he and Patsy melted away into the crowd.

We just stood there looking at each other, neither of us knowing how to open the conversation. Eventually I blurted out: 'I don't believe this. I nearly didn't come. I didn't know what to expect. I thought you'd be pug-ugly, but on first impressions you're bloody handsome.'

He roared with laughter. 'I've been standing here with my fingers crossed, hoping you didn't turn up,' he confessed. 'George said you were lovely, but I thought: "If she's so nice, what's she doing staying in on a Saturday night? She must be a right mutt." But when you walked in the door I thought: "Cor, what a result!" '

We hit it off straight away. We went on to the party and had a right good night. At the end of the evening I invited him back for coffee. As we walked in, there was my old dad sprawled on the settee snoring away. We went into the kitchen and I made the coffee. We started to have a little kiss and a cuddle and he tried to go a bit further. I fancied him like mad but I stopped him. Then Micky asked if he could take me out for a drink. I said: 'Yes. Yes, please!'

At one o'clock the following day he pulled up in a cab and took me to The Blind Beggar pub. I felt as if I had known him for ever, he was so easy to talk to. We spent the whole day together, then went straight out in the evening and had another blinding night.

Wherever we went, people were coming up to him and saying that they were glad to see him out. It was great. He was the centre of attraction, almost like a film star. He invited me to his house for tea on Tuesday night. I couldn't believe it! I had only been out with him for the weekend and already he was inviting me to have tea with his mum. I'd been with Terry four years and I'd never met any of his family.

When I told my mum she wasn't exactly over the moon about me going out with a crook. Even though I was brought up in the East End and had three brothers, I wasn't from a crooked family. That made my mum dubious about Micky, but as she said: 'At least he's single.'

So it was all arranged. Micky would pick me up from work on Tuesday.

All day Monday I was walking on air. I had clean forgotten that Terry was picking me up that night. As I walked out of the factory gate I heard him hooting his car horn, so I strolled over and dismissively responded with: 'Yeah?'

He got the needle instantly. 'What do you mean, Yeah?' he spat. 'Get in the car.'

My mind was made up.

'No, I'm not getting in the car,' I said firmly. 'I don't want to go out with you any more. I met someone else on Saturday night.' At this Terry went mad and we had a right old punch-up in the street. I ended up with the biggest black eye you've ever seen in your life.

The following night, when Micky rang, I told him about Terry and the black eye. He was livid and vowed to sort Terry out.

I was so self-conscious about the way I looked that I was reluctant to meet his family. Eventually he talked me round, but when I met his mum she took one look at my face and gasped: 'Oh my God in Heaven! You bastard, Micky, what did you do that for?'

He laughed: 'Mum, I didn't do it. Would I hit the girl? I only met her Saturday.'

His mother refused to listen. 'Is this what prison taught you?' she demanded.

'Mum,' he insisted, 'I didn't do it!'

She turned to me. 'Did he do it?'

I laughed and said no.

'I can't believe that,' she mumbled and went back to preparing the dinner.

Then his dad came in and roared: 'You bastard! You've done this to this girl.' He turned to me. 'How long have you known him?' he asked.

'Since Saturday, but he didn't do it,' I replied.

His father would not accept that my Micky didn't do it. 'You're knocking the girl about,' he yelled. 'You can see that's a fresh black eye. She's only been with you since Saturday. It must have been you.'

Micky began to lose his temper but his mother interrupted with the dinner. No sooner had we started eating than Micky's sister Maureen walked in and shrieked: 'Oh Micky, what have you done?'

At this Micky exploded with indignation and swore that he was not the culprit. 'I'm not having this,' he said. 'You're my girl now. Me and this Terry will have to sort this out.'

From then on I knew the score. Me and Micky were inseparable – but to this day his family still think that he gave me that shiner.

Within a few months we had moved into a bedsit in Leytonstone. Actually it wasn't a room, more like a garage extension. It was horrible. It didn't even have a window, just a big mural painted on the wall with curtains either side, like the one in Hilda Ogden's house in *Coronation Street*. But we were together, starry-eyed and bang in love and that was all that mattered.

Then a cousin of mine told me about a flat around the corner, above a launderette. The landlord was an Irishman with one arm. I'll never forget him. He was reluctant to let the flat, but when I told him about the mural he laughed and agreed to let us have the flat rent-free as long as I cleaned the launderette and made sure the door was locked at night.

We were happy there and it wasn't long before I fell pregnant with my first child.

Eventually we were evicted from the flat after Micky and his mates were larking about one Saturday afternoon. Some workmen had been doing a job in the launderette, fixing floorboards down with a staplegun. They had left the gun behind and Micky and his pals began to fire the small nails everywhere – through the windows, through the floor. One even went through the dry-cleaning machine and another just missed a customer's head. Not surprisingly the landlord threw us out when he heard.

We didn't have anywhere to live, so we both went back to lodge with our respective parents. Shortly afterwards, Micky was arrested for robbery and locked up for four years. My world had changed, but I knew the type of man Micky was when I became involved with him and I accepted him warts and all.

Good old Mum sorted me out. She got me a little flat around the corner, right at the top of an old tenement block, and paid £60 key money which was a lot in those days.

Soon I gave birth to my daughter Melanie and couldn't wait to show her off to Micky in Wandsworth Prison. He had never really wanted children, but he was over the moon with her when he saw her and immediately asked me to marry him. I was so happy. We applied to get married straight away at Wandsworth Register Office.

On the day of the wedding some spiteful person telephoned the prison anonymously to warn that the wedding was just a ruse to cover an escape attempt by Micky. Obviously the authorities couldn't take any chances, so the police re-routed all the traffic and Micky was handcuffed to a prison officer. They even tried to put a bag over his head but he wouldn't stand for that. His prison van was escorted by police cars at the front and the back. You would have thought he was serving forty-four years, not just four.

I wore a white mini-dress, my cousin Patsy loaned me a mink coat and I had my hair done up on top in curls with little daisies set in it. When we arrived at the Register Office there were armed police everywhere. It was complete madness. We weren't allowed any guests apart from my mum and dad and, of course, Melanie. We were all searched – even the baby.

The police refused to allow Micky to take the handcuffs off for the ceremony which was all over in a matter of minutes.

The Registrar said: 'You may kiss the bride.'

'Oh no he can't,' barked one of the prison officers as they whisked him off to jail again.

They told my dad that if we kept up with the prison van, we could have half-an-hour visit in the prison.

As we came out of the Register Office there were press and TV cameras everywhere. We climbed into my dad's old blue van and a reporter knocked on the window asking 'What have you got to say?'

My dad had the hump and gave him a right mouthful and sent him off with a flea in his ear. In all the wrong ways it was a memorable day.

That evening the wedding was on the telly and the next day it was in all the papers. It must have been an omen: the start of my marriage was on the news and the end of it was too.

4

GANGSTER'S MOLL

As soon as a major villain is jailed or, as in Micky's case, dies, his criminal 'firm' organises a benefit night to raise funds for the family. It was at Micky's benefit in the East End that I became re-acquainted with Ronnie Cook.

We had met once before when he arrived to pick up my Micky early one morning while I was cooking breakfast. I opened the door and there stood this tough, athletic-looking man dressed in a tracksuit and jogging on the spot. He came in and I cooked him egg on toast.

On the benefit night, Ron came up to me, passed on his condolences, and very politely asked permission to visit me the next day. I thought nothing more of it until he turned up at the house the following morning with a wad of cash and told me that if I needed anything, anything at all, I just had to ask.

Over the next couple of months I went a bit wild. Every night I went out drinking, and everywhere I went I kept bumping into Ronnie Cook – in places that I knew had never been his haunts before. We hit it off right from the start and it was strange really because he was the exact opposite of my Micky. They were like chalk and cheese.

Micky was always flamboyant, extrovert, smart – the man about town. Ronnie was very quiet and soberly dressed. People were wary of him. He had a reputation for being a hard man and nobody messed with him. I liked that, but with me he was always kind and gentle. He always seemed to have money and he started bringing me lots of presents. My Micky was a robber, but he wasn't in Ronnie's league. Ronnie was a top-of-the-tree robber, into heavy blags.

Over the next two years my life changed totally. I wanted for nothing, Ronnie made sure of that. He never gave me large amounts of money, but he took care of all my bills, I had the finest clothes that money could buy, and my kids never went without anything they wanted. He left his wife and moved in with a friend, but I saw him every day and we went out together most nights. Slowly, almost inevitably, I fell in love with him.

When, years later, I stood trial for murdering Ronnie, the prosecution suggested that my motive was an overwhelming desire to get my hands on his money. That was a joke. With Ron alive I never wanted for anything. But he was shrewd. He used to spread his money around and invested the bulk of it in legitimate businesses.

Ron confessed that he had fallen in love with me the very first morning he saw me, but forced the thought to the back of his mind because I was married to one of his friends. He never returned to the house again while Micky was alive because he was so ashamed. When he told me, I laughed my head off and said: 'I was dressed in my dressing gown with my hair in curlers and looking like something the cat dragged in. How could you fall in love with me?'

He replied: 'I don't know. There was something about you that looked so lovely. When Micky died, after the sorrow of losing him as a friend, I made it my aim in life to get you.'

Years later he explained that he used to hide and watch me leave the house and then guess by the direction I was taking where I was going, so that he could beat me there and be standing waiting for me with a drink. Bless him. He deserved eleven out of ten for effort. He certainly got me all right.

Ron treated me like a queen. He only let me have the best of the best. I only wore hand-made shoes, designer clothes, pure silk underwear and beautiful jewellery. I was always finding jewellery which he had hidden in my house as a kind of game. He was always buying me presents to make me smile. He never ever said 'No' to me. Ron gave me everything I ever wanted. He doted on me. Why would I wait ten years for him, only to kill him?

My whole affair with Ronnie began on a Saturday night just a few weeks after Micky's funeral. Gerry and his girlfriend took me out for a drink in The Carpenters Arms and Ron was in there with his wife Renee. He walked over, passed on his condolences, and asked if he could see me in private. We arranged an appointment for the following day at my mother's house in Stepney where I was living at the time.

When he arrived he explained that he had been to my old house several times but had missed me on each occasion. Then he simply handed me a huge wad of banknotes and mumbled something about being sure I could use the money. Before I could thank him properly he was gone, leaving me open-mouthed and my mother standing in the doorway with a cup of tea she had poured for him.

The following Sunday night I was having a drink in The Needlegun in the Roman Road with my sister-in-law Maureen, my mother-in-law and my brother Richard when who should stroll in but Ron. 'Look. That's that Ronnie Cook who came round to my mum's and gave me all that money,' I said to Maureen. She had recognised him but didn't know his name. He walked over, bought us all a drink, and told me that he had bought tickets for the benefit night being held in Romford.

'Where's your handbag?' he asked, all of a sudden. I pointed it out, lying on the bar, and he scolded me saying: 'You shouldn't leave it there, somebody might nick it.' I just giggled and told him there was nothing worth nicking in it. With that he got up and bought us all another drink.

When he returned from the bar he asked me: 'Have you bought your outfit for the benefit yet?' I told him that I couldn't afford a great deal and he smiled and said: 'Well, if you find that you get a sudden windfall buy yourself something nice for it,' and as quietly as he had arrived he got up and left.

Half-an-hour later, when it was my turn to buy the drinks, I found £600 – a lot of money in 1979 – stuffed into my handbag.

'There's your sudden windfall,' said Maureen. 'You heard what the man said, go and buy yourself something special.'

So, like an excited schoolgirl, I went out shopping and bought a black chiffon two-piece suit. The skirt was plain black with just two fine lines of gold thread running around the hem. The top was like a camisole underneath and the overtop had long sleeves with a little frill round the cuffs and a soft frill round the neck. The frills were also decorated with two fine lines of gold thread. It cost £175 and was the most expensive item of clothing I had ever bought.

I added a beautiful pair of black high-heels which, at £85, were the dearest shoes I had ever bought in my life.

On the night of the first benefit I felt so elegant. I stood at the door with Maureen and the organiser to welcome the guests. At about ten o'clock Ronnie walked in on his own.

'You look beautiful,' he said. 'I can see from the outfit that you got that windfall. This is for you to complete the stunning effect.' He handed me a bottle of Chanel No5, winked, and walked on into the hall.

'That Ronnie Cook fancies you,' said Maureen. When I argued that he was just being kind because of Micky's memory she added: 'I know the look of a man who's got the hots. You wait and see!'

The benefit went very well. Everyone was being extremely generous, buying raffle tickets and bidding for items in the auction. When it came to the bottle of champagne the bids steadily rose to £200 until a gruff voice boomed out: 'One thousand pounds.' Everyone looked round to see who had made such an outrageous bid. It was Ronnie Cook. Pulling £1,000 cash from his pocket he slapped the money on the auctioneer's table and simply said: 'Re-auction it!' Then he strode over to me and said: 'I'm glad it's going so well for you. If I don't see you before, I've bought tickets for the second benefit in a fortnight's time. Goodnight.' And he walked out.

Maureen smiled at me. 'What have you got to say now?' she asked. 'He's *definitely* got the hots for you.'

I had to admit, this Ronnie Cook was beginning to intrigue me.

The next weekend I was out drinking in The Carpenters Arms with my brother Richard when, once again, in breezed Ronnie.

'Your sister looked gorgeous at the benefit last week,' he said to Richard. I smiled and said, 'I think the clothes had a lot to do with it. Actually, I bought them out of a windfall I had.'

'And what have you bought for next week?' he asked. 'Surely it must be even nicer.'

I said that I was planning to wear the same outfit, but when my brother later went to the toilet Ron shoved £200 into my hand and begged, 'Buy something new for next week, please. You deserve it.'

I was overcome. I stammered something about how grateful I was and how he didn't need to do it but he simply said, 'I know. I want to.'

A little later another of my girlfriends joined us and I told her that Ronnie had given me Chanel No5 at the benefit.

'Only the best is good enough for you,' he said, 'and you deserve the dearest.'

'That was a really nice thought,' said my girlfriend, 'but Chanel No5 isn't the dearest perfume. Joy is.' I was very embarrassed and protested that Chanel was certainly good enough for me any day.

The following weekend was the second and bigger of the two benefit nights held in the East End. I had bought a beautiful black hand-crocheted dress, which was very flattering, and wore the same shoes as for the first benefit. I felt like a million dollars.

Once again I stood in the entrance with one of the organisers, a man called John. Again Ronnie walked in on his own, told me I looked lovely, and handed me a bottle of Joy. I laughed, thanked him, and kissed him on the cheek.

John seemed a little taken aback. 'Hello Ron, lovely to see you here mate,' he said. When Ron had passed on into the hall John turned to me and said, 'I had no idea you knew Ronnie Cook.' I explained that I hardly knew him at all and put John in the picture.

'Well he usually doesn't come to these sort of things because of the Old Bill,' said John.

'Why would he be bothered about the police?' I asked.

'Because of what he does for a living,' replied John.

'Well I got the impression that he was a crook,' I said, 'but then so is almost everybody here tonight.'

'Ah, but there aren't many who are top of the tree like Ronnie,' said John. 'He's one of the best . . . and one of the most careful.'

When it came to the auction Ron went through the same routine, paying £1,000 for a case of vodka which he ordered should be re-auctioned, 'but this time I got a kiss on the cheek and a whispered: 'You're beautiful, do you know that?' before he slipped away.

A few days later he appeared unexpectedly in The Needlegun while Maureen and I were there and asked if he could take the two of us out for a drink. He drove us across the river to The Swan and Sugarloaf pub in south Croydon where I met the Arif brothers for the first time. Another of the top criminals in the group that night was utterly charming and kept insisting that we drink pink champagne. We had a lovely evening and Ronnie behaved like a perfect gentleman and dropped us off at Maureen's house in Bow.

Within days he had asked if I would go out with him, but my brother Richard refused to let me go unaccompanied because Micky had only been dead four months and he was concerned that people might talk. So for over a week the three of us went out together every night. Ron was very polite and patient about the situation, but it did make me laugh. Richard was my younger brother and here he was chaperoning me. He even insisted on me going indoors with him at the end of each evening and as I was living at my mother's house I had no choice.

When it came to the Friday night Ronnie asked, 'Will I be seeing you both tomorrow night?'

'You'll be seeing me but you won't be seeing Richard. I think we are old enough to go out on our own. Don't you?' I replied.

He took me to meet a friend of his who owned The Black Lion pub in Epping. When he was told who I was, the friend commiserated and said, 'I guessed you had lost somebody dear to you because you are dressed in black from head to toe.' I explained that I intended to wear black until my next birthday.

'When's you birthday, Sweetheart?' asked Ron innocently. When I told him it was a week later he said, 'Leave the arrangements up to me and forget it until the day.'

On the morning of my birthday, I was upstairs getting the kids ready for school when my mum called out: 'There's a flower van pulled up outside. I expect it's for you girl.' I ran down to open the door and the man said: 'Linda Calvey? Somebody must really love you.' He handed me two huge bouquets of roses, but when I thanked him he said: 'That's just the start, Love. Your boyfriend's ordered you 200!'

I left my mum struggling to find places for all the flowers as I took the children to school and when I got back Ronnie was there, beaming all over his face. He was planning to take me out that evening and, knowing that I had pledged to stop wearing black on my birthday, he had bought me a new outfit for the occasion. He had secretly asked my mother for my clothing size and he had an array of bags with him. 'I didn't buy you underwear in case they thought I was a nonce,' he said, 'but I bought you the rest.'

There was a pair of the most lovely cream and bronze high-heels and a matching bag – a tiny thing with a long, thin strap and a bronze flower on the front. The dress was the most beautiful garment I've ever seen. It was cream silk chiffon, off the shoulder, with rows of crystal, silver and gold beads hanging in fringing down the front.

I ran upstairs and put the dress on. It felt like something Marilyn Monroe might wear, and I nearly cried. I couldn't believe how happy I was feeling. Ronnie was thrilled too. 'You look like a film star, Babe,' he said. 'Go and get your hair done and I'll be back to take you out for a meal.'

'If you wait 'til I change, you can run me to the hairdresser's,' I said.

'Run yourself,' he replied.

'I can't. I don't have a car,' I said.

'Haven't you? Well, who does that brown Mini belong to?' he asked.

I looked outside.

'These keys and documents say the car belongs to you,' grinned Ronnie. 'It is also taxed and insured so, as I say, take yourself to the hairdresser's.'

I was speechless. I had never met anyone so generous before. I was like a little kid in a toyshop.

That evening when he arrived to pick me up I kissed him and said: 'Thank you. I am so lucky to have you.'

'No, Princess, I am lucky to have you,' he replied with a serious tone in his voice.

He took me to a restaurant in Winchmore Hill, which was full of all my friends, and arranged several surprises like a huge birthday cake and a group of singing waiters to serenade me. It was the best birthday I had ever had in my whole life.

When we got home I made a coffee and as we sat in the lounge I said to Ron: 'Thank you, thank you, thank you for the best day of my life!'

'But I haven't given you your birthday present yet,' he replied.

'Yes you have,' I said. 'The flowers, the shoes, the bag, the dress, tonight, and my beautiful car – surely they are my birthday presents.'

'Well partly,' he said, 'but here is your main present. Come and sit down next to me and close your eyes.'

He held my hand, gently took off my wedding and engagement rings, put them on to my right hand and slid another ring on to my left hand. When I opened my eyes, there was a gorgeous diamond cluster ring.

'Now you've got your present,' he said.

Who would have thought that my life could have changed so much, so soon? I was so happy, I was walking on air.

Three weeks later I went on holiday with my family to Majorca – a break my parents had planned and booked soon after Micky died. On the first night I telephoned Ron and told him how much I missed him and how quiet Majorca was without him. The next afternoon he turned up at the hotel.

That evening we went for a long walk in the warm night air. Ron turned to me, put his hands on my shoulders and said, 'Linda, I have looked for somebody like you all my life. You are my life. You are all I want to be with.'

After that, we couldn't stay away from one another for a moment. We were together night and day. I didn't want the holiday to end.

When we got home there was a letter waiting for me to view a flat the following day. Because of the hate mail I'd been getting the council were going to re-house me.

The flat was fine and we had to move in straight away, so my sisters and I went over to the old house and began to pack things up. We'd not been working long when there was a knock at the door and there stood Ronnie.

'Listen, Angel,' he said, 'I want you to have a completely fresh start, so just keep your clothes and the kids' clothes and toys and give everything else away. I will buy you everything new.'

When I protested at the cost he simply said, 'I love to see you happy. Don't even pack a teaspoon. Give everything away.'

You can imagine how pleased I was. Even though my furniture was lovely, the thought of getting everything new was really exciting. I gave it all to my family. I kept just two items – the JVC stack system Micky had recently purchased and an old-fashioned wooden telephone he had bought a few years earlier.

When 61 Pembroke Road had been cleared, I gave back the keys of the house that Micky had walked out of that fateful December day. I finally felt that all the sadness was behind me.

Ronnie paid for the new flat to be decorated throughout. I had seen a picture of an old-fashioned fireplace so Ron had one built out of old beams from a church. We ordered curtains, blinds and carpets and bought new crystal chandeliers. Then we went and picked out beds, bedroom suites, a three-piece suite, cabinets, a TV, kitchen utensils, bedding and all the little knick-knacks that make a house a home. It was perfect when it was finished.

We hadn't spoken about Ron living with me until the flat was ready, but when I asked him, he said he had too much respect for me to move in so quickly. However, he couldn't bear living two lives, so he moved out of his home and went to live with his friend Griff, just around the corner from my new flat.

* * *

Throughout the sordid saga of Linda's love affair with Ronnie Cook, his forgotten wife Renee was the most unfortunate victim. While her husband was lavishing vast amounts of money on his lover, his wife could barely afford the cost of clothing or food for herself and their three children. The cruellest twist came four years after Cook's death, when the Criminal Injuries Compensation board refused her application for compensation following his murder on the grounds of his 'bad character'. The High Court later endorsed that decision.

Linda continues:

After I moved out of my mother's house, I confessed to her and to the kids that Ronnie was a married man. They were all horrified and, although they liked Ron very much and couldn't do anything about it, they made it clear that they deeply disapproved of what we were doing.

Once Ron had left his wife we began to go out very regularly. Gradually I got involved in his circle of friends – all lovely people – but what a rogues' gallery they turned out to be. Our Friday night routine was always the same – a trip to south London. First we went to 'Flash' Harry's – he was a friend of Ronnie who owned The Harp of Erin – and then on to The Swan and Sugarloaf in south Croydon to drink with 'Scatts' Tobin, Osar and Dogan Arif, John 'Little Legs' Lloyd and John 'Goldfinger' Fleming who was later extradited from South America to England to face charges over the Brinks Mat gold bullion robbery. I also became very close to Annie Marks, the widow of 'Ginger' Marks who was shot by Freddie Foreman's gang in the East End one night, bundled into a car and never seen again. We obviously had something in common.

In fact the company Linda was keeping on these Friday night jaunts represented the absolute cream of the British criminal establishment at the time.

'Flash' Harry Hayward was a member of the Hayward family which ruled south London gangland along with the notorious Richardson brothers. His brother Billy was one of the men convicted after the infamous gunfight and murder of a Kray gang member at Mr Smith's Club in Catford.

Billy 'Scatts' Tobin ran the so-called 'Thursday Gang' which specialised in hijacking security vans in the south-east London area, often with considerable violence. On one occasion one of his lieutenants James Moody, dressed as a policeman, jumped out of a car in the Blackwall Tunnel and forced a security van to stop. To prevent the alarm being raised he took the keys from a number of nearby motorists. In 1978 Tobin was acquitted on ten counts of conspiracy to rob and possession of firearms with intent in relation to the £197,000 raid at the *Daily Mirror* offices during which a security guard was shot. In this case, Tobin alleged he had paid Hugh Moore, later Assistant Chief Constable for the City of London Police, for help. The allegation led to the notorious police corruption investigation, Operation Countryman, which, after years of inquiries and millions of pounds of public money had been spent, found no police wrongdoing.

The Arif family, six brothers of Turkish Cypriot extraction, ran a huge slice of illegality in south London. 'It doesn't matter whose name is over the door of the pub in some areas,' said one police officer, 'it's the Arifs who own it.' Pubs, restaurants and clubs were bought by the Arifs with the proceeds from major armed robberies. Dogan Arif, who later went to prison for fourteen years for his part in an £8.5 million drug-smuggling plot, was the owner and chairman of a football club, non-league Fisher Athletic, which spent vast sums on buying well-known players and even had the flamboyant Malcolm Allison as its manager, although there was never any wrongdoing associated with the club or with Allison himself.

John Fleming was chased around the world by detectives

investigating the record-breaking Brinks Mat gold bullion robbery at London's Heathrow Airport. Deported from Florida in 1986 and facing allegations from a supergrass, Fleming was charged with dishonestly handling £500,000 proceeds of the robbery, but the court found he had no case to answer.

Meanwhile Linda and her lover were beginning to establish a very cosy relationship:

My parents always had the kids over the weekend and Ronnie and me had a right good old time. Then, we went on holiday to Corfu with Terry Marks, 'Ginger' Marks's brother, and his partner and another young couple. Ronnie took me to Harrods to shop for the holiday, but for himself only bought a couple of pairs of swimming trunks. While we were in Corfu, Ron was introduced to smoking dope. He was such a fitness fanatic that he'd never smoked anything at all, but he enjoyed the feeling it gave him and after that used cannabis quite regularly.

When it came to his birthday, I decided I wanted to make it as special for him as he had made mine for me. He didn't wear any jewellery, so I bought him a gold Omega watch. I also had a crystal whisky tumbler engraved with the inscription 'Happy Birthday Ronnie – 24th July'. Then I organised a surprise party for him with all his friends and all the East End fare – jellied eels, prawns, the lot – and, of course, a well-stocked bar. I had a few scares getting him there without him guessing what was going on, but in the end it was a fantastic party that went on until the early hours.

All the way home Ronnie said, 'Thanks for the best party I have ever had in my life. No, correction, thanks for not only the best party but the only party anyone has ever laid on for me in my life. You spoil me.'

I had earlier given him the whisky tumbler, so when we got home I went through the same main present routine he had done with me. He opened the box with the watch in it, closed it again and said, 'It's beautiful, but I don't wear watches. If I wanted to I could buy the most expensive watch in the world. I would be much happier if you took it back and exchanged it for something you could wear. *You* should wear the jewellery.'

I was obviously upset, so he agreed to wear the watch when he left, but said that he loved the glass and that was all he really wanted.

The next day when he came round he was wearing a child's toy Mickey Mouse watch. 'I wanted to make a point, Darling,' he said. 'If I wanted, I could wear the cheapest to the dearest, but I hate wearing any watches or jewellery, so please take it back and change it for something for yourself.'

I just burst into tears and blurted out, 'I only wanted to make you happy and I've done it all wrong.'

Gently he took me in his arms, kissed my eyes and said, 'Princess, you have made me happier than I ever imagined it was possible to be. I am sorry I made you cry. For you I will wear it from now on.'

He left and came back later that day. He told me to sit on his lap and close my eyes. When I opened them he had put a thick gold choker chain around my neck as an apology for making me cry. After that he wore the watch but kept it on in the steam-room he went to twice a week, and it eventually went wrong when he went swimming with it on. He never got it repaired.

Although he never lived with me, Ronnie always put £100 on my mantelpiece every Friday night for my housekeeping – a small fortune in 1979 – and also paid all my bills – electricity, gas, telephone, car tax and all the clothing for me and the kids. He was the most generous man I have ever met.

Every Saturday we had the same routine. Ronnie would come straight to my flat from his jogging. I would run him a bath and put his jogging clothes into the washing machine to wash and dry. Then we would go to bed for an hour or so and afterwards he would put on the only article of clothing he kept at my flat – a towelling robe.

Then he would settle down in front of the television to watch the racing with the telephone next to him. He telephoned his bets to the bookie and only ever bet to win, always gambling between £3,000 and £5,000. He lost more often than he won, but he said it was his only vice, apart from me, and he would never gamble what he couldn't afford to lose. I cooked him fillet steak, chips and peas – the only meal I ever used to cook him – and he always joked that I was the most expensive restaurant in town.

Our Saturday evenings were routine too. I went to the hairdresser late in the afternoon while Ronnie went home to change. Then we would go to a very classy restaurant in Camden Passage. Most of the customers were there for special occasions and stayed all evening, but we would eat in about an hour and go on elsewhere. After we'd been going there for several weeks the manager suggested that we take a regular booking and he would telephone us each Thursday to take our advance order. 'Who shall I ask for?' he inquired. 'Just ask for Madame Harpley,' said Ron with a giggle. Harpley was the name of my block of flats.

One night the arrangement almost backfired. Both Ronnie and I had ordered lobster thermidor, fresh not frozen. As he was taking us to our table the manager said, 'It's lucky I phoned you because I was only able to get two lobsters today, but they are reserved for you.'

When our main course arrived, a posh man with a very loud voice shouted out, 'Manager, how dare you tell me that you have no lobster and then serve two people who arrived after me with the meal I required?'

The manager was very apologetic. 'Please Sir, don't make a scene,' he said. 'It is true we haven't any lobsters, only those two and they were ordered in advance by Madame Harpley.'

'Well, how come I wasn't asked when I booked if I'd like anything special?' he continued. He obviously thought the restaurant was too expensive for us to have a regular weekly booking. 'What have these people got that we haven't?' he bellowed.

Ronnie was beginning to get wound up so I looked across at big mouth and said, 'I'll tell you what we've got, pal. We've got manners and plenty of dough.'

'Come on, Angel, let's skip the sweet tonight,' said Ron and we left. In the car he said, 'I hate people showing off about what they have. He deserved what you said. Posh prat. I bet he only had a fiver and a credit card in his pocket.' It was the only time I ever heard Ronnie say anything about how much he had. He was never, ever, flash that way.

I knew that Ronnie was getting fed up with living at Griff's. It was only a tiny mobile home shared by Griff, his wife Kathy, their daughter Debbie and three dogs. With Ron there, too, it was very cramped. Every week he went to his wife's house to give her her wages and to spend a couple of hours with his son Ronnie junior whom he adored and missed terribly.

One day he asked if he could borrow my mini. When he came back later, he had bought me a bright yellow VW Golf with a black-and-white checked interior as a surprise. That night over dinner he admitted that the car was a peace offering because he wanted to go back and live at home and he was afraid of my reaction. He promised that the move was only for comfort and to be near his children who were begging him to spend more time with them. It was temporary until we could get married, he promised. He was going to sleep in the spare room and our life together would be unaffected.

I said, 'Look, I have the best of both worlds. I have my children who I adore living with me, plus you to love and to love me too. I am no hypocrite. I know you love your children. As long as I see you as much, I don't mind.'

'You're a diamond, Princess,' he said. 'I really thought you would say no and if you had I would have gone back to Griff's because you are my life and I couldn't ever be without you.'

When it came to Christmas that year I bought Ron a couple of cashmere jumpers, having learned my lesson with the gold watch. He gave me a silver fox bolero and a three-colour gold bracelet along with £1,000 cash. He also bought a portable TV for Melanie and a new bike for Neil.

During the Old Year's Night celebrations I reflected on the contrast between that Christmas and the sadness of the previous year. My life had changed so dramatically for the better inside twelve months and it still did not seem real.

Early in 1980 we met some friends who were planning a trip to Las Vegas to watch the Muhammad Ali fight at Caesar's Palace. Ronnie decided it would be fun to join them so we began to make the arrangements. One day Ronnie came round to my flat with a plastic carrier bag, all rolled up.

'What's that, a present for me?' I asked.

'Indirectly, yes,' he said, opening the package which contained a pile of American dollars.

'Oh, the holiday money,' I said. 'Do you want me to mind it for you?'

But Ronnie wanted to find somewhere else to leave the cash. I was offended and accused him of not trusting me. He just laughed and said, 'Princess, I trust you more than anyone, but this wasn't drawn from a bank in the conventional way.'

He'd never discussed with me what he did for a living, but I knew that he had the reputation as one of the top blaggers in the country so I just casually replied, 'Ah, you mean it is the proceeds of a robbery.'

'Yeah,' he said. 'When the cash was being sorted out there was this American money, so I said I would have it in my share because we were going over there in a couple of weeks' time and it would save changing money at the airport.'

We decided to leave the package with my friend Nita who lived in the next block of flats. She put it in a drawer and didn't ask any questions. When we left, Ronnie said, 'I am happier it's there with Nita because she's never had any problems with the police and she's got two dogs to scare off any burglars.'

Two days later there was a very loud banging on my door early in the morning. When I answered it in my dressing gown there stood two policeman. One of them was holding the carrier bag.

'Can I help you?' I asked.

They looked a bit embarrassed and one said, 'Well, I don't know if you can or not, really. We had a warrant to search a flat across the way for stolen jewellery, but we didn't find any. Instead we found this.'

He thrust the bag out in front of him and added, 'The lady said it belongs to you, but I expect you don't know anything about it.'

'Yes, it's mine,' I said firmly.

'But we haven't told you what's in it yet,' said the policeman.

'You don't need to. It's American dollars and they're mine,' I said.

The officers began shuffling their feet. They had no warrant to search my house and they clearly didn't know what to do.

'You'd better come in. Do you want a cup of tea?' I asked, smiling sweetly.

They borrowed my phone to ring Nita's flat and speak to their boss who soon came over to join them. They were ever so polite and I made them tea and allowed them to search my flat even though they had no warrant. Then came the inevitable question. Where did the money come from?

'It came from an armed robbery I expect,' I said with a straight face.

'I beg your pardon,' said the senior officer, 'did you say armed robbery?'

'Yes,' I said. 'I don't think you have realised who I am yet. I am Michael Calvey's widow.'

'Oh, your husband was the bloke shot dead during the blag in south London. By all accounts he was a really nice bloke. I'm sorry about that,' said the officer, 'but what has that got to do with this money?'

'I wanted to put a couple of hooks up in the kitchen and I got Micky's toolbox out,' I said. 'When I opened it I found this bag of money.'

'But he's been dead over a year,' said the detective.

'Yes, but I am a woman,' I said, 'how often would your wife open a toolbox? I was so surprised I took it over to Nita's to show her and left it there while I decided what to do with it.'

The police believed me and took Nita and me down to the police station where they took statements from us in a comfortable waiting room and told us we would need to come back in twenty-eight days, by which time they were confident it would all be sorted out.

Nita was distraught. 'I am so sorry I said it was yours,' she sobbed. 'I was so frightened I didn't know what to say.'

I reassured her and praised her for not mentioning Ronnie. I told her to stick to the story that I had taken the money to her and never to mention that I was going to America with my boyfriend.

When I caught up with Ronnie he was horrified.

'What were they doing searching Nita's, she's totally straight?' he asked. 'I can't stand to think I've got you involved with the Old Bill, after all you've been through with Micky's death. Why did you say the money was yours?'

'Better for me to get nicked than you,' I replied. 'Don't look on the black side, Babe, when I go back in twenty-eight days' time they'll probably drop it.'

He just shook his head and looked grim. 'I don't think you'll have to wait that long,' he said. 'When I steal British currency I go through it carefully and destroy any note which has the slightest mark on it that could identify the batch it came from. In this case, because it was US dollars and we were spending it abroad I didn't check. It only takes one note to have any marking and it will pinpoint exactly where it came from.'

I laughed it off but he was deadly serious. 'I've got a gut feeling they will be back and this time they won't be polite,' he said. 'Princess, you don't know what it is like. They will put you in a cell and drive you crazy trying to get things out of you.'

I was still upbeat and assured him that it was better I be arrested than him because, although my Micky was a known armed robber, I had a clean record, whereas he had only just won an appeal against a fourteen-year sentence for armed robbery and the police were determined to get him.

The next day there was a loud banging on the door and there were the heavy mob. No friendly conversation over a cup of tea this time. 'You think you are so clever with that crap story you gave the local Old Bill,' said one. 'Well, you might have had them over but we are not so easy to fool. Get your coat, you're nicked.'

At the police station the atmosphere was hostile and nasty. A couple of the notes had marks on them that proved they had been stolen during a robbery in London's West End. In the course of that robbery, outside a bank in The Strand, a security guard had been shot.

The detectives kept telling me that not co-operating would go against me in court. The only clue they had which linked back to the robbery gang was me. 'Look, we know that your old man was an armed robber and we know you are covering up. Tell us whose money it is and who gave it to you,' they said. 'Don't you realise you are keeping these vicious thugs on the street?'

'Yes, and who made them vicious?' I replied, 'You lot when you murdered my husband. The money is mine. You won't get anything out of me.'

The police really had the hump but they knew I wouldn't talk, so they charged both Nita and me with dishonestly handling the proceeds of an armed robbery.

It was 9 September 1980 and because of the dramatic death of her husband Linda was newsworthy. Under the headline '4 on currency charges' the *Daily Telegraph*'s two-paragraph report read:

> Linda Calvey, 32, widow of Michael Calvey, shot dead by a detective during an attempted armed raid in 1978, and three other people were charged last night with dishonestly handling foreign currency.
>
> Mrs Calvey of Globe Road, Stepney, Brian Crooks, publican of Pedro Street Clapton, Alan Gentry, 45, unemployed of Boundary Road, Walthamstow, and Anita Karstadt, 40, also unemployed of Norfolk Estate, Stepney will appear at Hendon tomorrow.

Linda takes up the story:

They held us both for a couple of days until our court appearance. Whenever the officers spoke to me they told me that Nita could not stop crying and tried to make me feel guilty for getting her involved. Of course I felt desperately sorry for Nita, but I was far too loyal to Ronnie ever to say anything that might have led them to him.

Ronnie told me to plead guilty and think up a moody story as to how I got the money. As a first-time offender, he said, they'd never send me to prison. All Nita had to do was to plead guilty to dishonestly handling stolen goods and say that she had believed my story about finding the money in a toolbox and foolishly agreed to help me out by looking after it. That way she should surely avoid any come-backs.

Ronnie came up with a perfect story for me to tell in court. I would say that when Micky died my standard of living had dropped dramatically and, as a young widow with two small children, I had no means of making ends meet. So, faced with this desperate predicament, I decided to make some quick money by becoming a high-class prostitute.

The story was that I was working a top London hotel one night and went with an American client called Hank. He agreed to pay my fee of £500, although he thought it a bit steep, and while we were having a drink in his hotel room afterwards he began to question me about why I had turned to prostitution. I seemed a bit naïve for a hooker and he didn't think I had been on the game for very long.

Then, so my alibi went, I told him the whole story of my misfortune and he opened his briefcase saying, as he handed me the bundle of stolen dollars, 'Sweetheart, you've touched my heart. Take this.' Having now discovered the origin of the money, I would say, I could understand why my story had touched his heart because, like my Micky, he was obviously an armed robber too.

On the day of the trial I realised that I would have to play up to the role of a high-class prostitute so I dressed for the part. I put on a white silk shirt and a long tartan kilt over riding boots with a fur jacket – the whole effect was smart but just a touch tarty.

When we got to court we bumped into some of the heavy mob – the Robbery Squad detectives. One of them said to me, 'Cor, they'll love you in Holloway, all dressed up like that!'

I just winked at him and said, 'I'm not going to Holloway. I was thinking more of Hawaii.'

One of his colleagues laughed. 'You ain't going home, Sweetheart,' he said.

Right up until that point I had refused to plead guilty so the police were shocked when I stood in the box and did.

When the judge asked for my mitigation I launched into the false story I had rehearsed. The police looked at me with disbelief and when I said my client's name was Hank one of them stifled a snigger. I could imagine them thinking 'Hank the Yank? Yeah, right!'

The prosecution said that because of my refusal to co-operate, none of the gang members involved in what had turned out to be a very nasty crime had been traced.

At this point the judge retired to consider the matter. When he returned, the police in court grinned at me and several of them gave me the thumbs-down signal in the Roman gladiator style.

After a long lecture the judge told me that he believed my story but, because of the seriousness of the crime, he felt that a custodial sentence of two years would be appropriate for both Nita and me.

Well, Nita burst into tears and I glanced at the police who were looking sick as pigs. They wanted a much longer sentence than two years. I was in a daze because I had made no arrangements for my children. I felt so deflated, having been so flash outside the court boasting that I was going to Hawaii instead of Holloway prison. Then, to my delight, at the very end of his speech the judge said that he was taking into account the fact that we were both of previous good character. He felt compassion for both of us. My children, he said, had been traumatised by the death of their father and he did not want to punish them by taking their mother away from them. He was suspending the sentence for a year, he said.

The Old Bill nearly fell off their seats with shock.

We both thanked the judge for his leniency and he leaned forward in a very avuncular manner. 'By the way, Mrs Calvey,' he said, 'please reconsider and think very carefully before you take up that profession. There's a lot of very nasty people out there and you could easily come unstuck.'

Despite getting suspended sentences we both also got heavy fines, but Ronnie arranged to have them paid for us. He was gutted that I now had a criminal record thanks to him, but hugely proud of me for my loyalty to him. 'Princess, I will never forgive myself for this,' he said.

In the middle of all this, while I was on bail from the magistrates court and before Nita and I went to trial at Acton Crown Court, Ronnie and I went on the holiday to Las Vegas which had been the cause of all the trouble.

We both fell in love with the place the moment we got off the plane. Las Vegas is a fairyland for grownups. Everything is dedicated to your comfort. I've never seen so many fruit machines. Nothing ever closes and everything revolves around the gaming tables.

Ronnie had brought £28,000 with him. It was a hell of a lot of money to spend on a two-week holiday in 1980, but he said he never spent more than he could afford and as he had always wanted to see Las Vegas he had no intention of scrimping.

We lived in the lap of luxury on that holiday. The best cabaret acts in the world were on display and every night we went to a different show. Our favourite was a magic show where people were changed into wild animals – lions and tigers. We were amazed when an elephant was brought on to the stage and made to disappear before our eyes.

The Ali fight took place at Caesar's Palace where we found ourselves rubbing shoulders with a host of stars. I immediately recognised the man sitting behind us. It was the good-looking dark-haired actor Erik Estrada who played Poncherello, the traffic cop in the TV show *CHiPs*. He was with a really loud ignorant sort of American bimbo who kept complaining that people like us were sitting in front of them when we weren't celebrities. Eventually this got too much for Ron. He turned round and said: 'Listen Darling, we may not be famous, but we've got a helluva lot more money than you, so that's why we've got better seats. All right?'

That shut her up and you could see that Erik Estrada was really embarrassed. I was a bit surprised because it wasn't like Ronnie at all. He was never flash or boastful about his money and usually kept very quiet in public. He usually left the talking to me. Anyway, the atmosphere was electric and even though Ali lost it was a truly memorable night.

Ronnie bought me a beautiful handbag that was made of feathers. He joked that it was so unusual that by the time we got home they would probably be selling them down at the East End's Roman Road market, but to this day I have never seen anything like it anywhere.

Las Vegas, of course, is full of wedding chapels. I wanted to see inside one of them but Ronnie said, 'No way. If I go inside one of those chapels you might capture me.'

I replied: 'I can't capture you, you are still married.'

On the plane coming home he said, 'Princess, one day I promise I will marry you and when I do we'll come back to Las Vegas and get married in one of those little chapels.' I was over the moon with happiness and flew back all the way to England in a daze of joy.

As the year progressed Ronnie began to talk more and more about a good friend of his called Brian Thorogood, who had just finished a fifteen-year sentence for armed robbery. Before he went away, Brian had invested money with a friend in a haulage, warehousing and shipping agent's firm. It had grown into a large and very successful concern while Brian was in jail and Ronnie asked to buy into the company. However, the other directors weren't happy about having another crook for a partner, so Ron's friend set up a subsidiary which was a haulage company owned solely by himself and Ronnie.

One day Ronnie said to me, 'Let's get Nita on a blind date with my friend Brian. It will do him good to have a good night out.' Nita and I both agreed, but on the appointed night Brian didn't show up. He made an excuse about having to work late, so the date was re-arranged for the following Friday night. He was dreadfully late and we were about to leave the pub when he finally showed up, almost an hour after he had been expected.

I had never met him before, but I was so angry on behalf of Nita that I gave him a right mouthful. Nita asked me to be nice to him because she quite liked him, so I buttoned my lip for the rest of the evening, but he and I just did not hit it off from the very start. What happened next, though, made Ron and me laugh our heads off every time we thought of it afterwards.

At the end of the evening Nita invited Brian in to her place for a coffee and told him she was just going to slip into something more comfortable. He thought she was going to change her shoes for slippers or something like that and was shocked when she reappeared wearing a negligee and sexy underwear. According to him, she was very amorous with him but he was not at all amorous in return and could not wait to make his excuses and leave.

Not knowing any of this, I telephoned Nita the next morning to ask how she and Brian had got on.

'I think he must be a poof,' she said. 'I put all my sexy underwear on and he clammed up like a fish. He couldn't wait to get out of my house.'

When Ronnie heard this he rang Brian and asked how he had got on with Nita.

'She's a raving nymphomaniac,' he grunted. 'She's a nice enough lady, but not for me.'

'Saucy bastard,' I yelled. 'Who did he want then, Liz Taylor? He wasn't exactly the life and soul of the party himself.'

Ronnie laughed. 'Princess, I'm really surprised you and him didn't hit it off. He's a lovely man if you get to know him.'

'It's all right, I can do without knowing him, thank you,' I snapped.

How ironic that exchange was in retrospect, considering the relationship that was later to develop between Brian and me.

5

CHRISTMAS STOCKING

That year flew by and once again it was December. I had bought all the presents and made all the arrangements early and Ronnie had taken me on a monumental spending spree to buy a whole new wardrobe of classy and expensive yuletide clothes. Everything was set fair for another lovely Christmas.

On 14 December – I'll never forget the date – Ronnie took me out for a meal, but he was very quiet and totally preoccupied throughout the evening. When we got home I nagged him to tell me what was troubling him. At first he was reluctant, but eventually he relented and said it was 'work'.

I knew that 'work' meant an armed robbery and that made me very upset. 'Not this month Ronnie, not December,' I begged. 'I can't stand it. December is such a bad month. It's unlucky for that sort of thing. Micky died at Christmas.'

'I haven't committed myself yet but Scatts is driving me mad to go on this bit of work,' he said.

Scatts was Billy Tobin, one of his south London friends with whom we drank regularly in The Swan and Sugarloaf. I liked him. He was a really nice man – a bit flash, maybe, but it suited him.

'It's a good prize,' said Ronnie. 'I will get between £200,000 and £250,000 as my share.'

'Do you need the money?' I asked.

'I don't need it,' he said, 'although you can never have too much money, but as you are so concerned, when I go to the meet tomorrow I'll say I don't fancy it.'

The following night he made an elaborate show of giving me a fabulous diamond ring as an early Christmas present. Then, just before he left, he sat me on his lap and confessed that he had agreed to take the bit of 'work' with Scatts. 'The others in the team asked me just to listen to the plan before I said no,' he said. 'They trusted me with their plans, so I tossed up my honour against my promise to you and I felt I just couldn't let them down.'

I burst into tears.

'So this ring isn't really my pre-Christmas present. It's to sweeten me up, isn't it?' I sobbed.

He wiped away my tears with tissues and gently said, 'Princess, I hate to see you cry. I know how you feel about December, but I had no choice. It will be all over tomorrow and then you can go and book us a holiday for January.'

Learning that the robbery was so soon made me even more apprehensive and I pleaded with him not to go.

'Princess, you are confusing me with Micky,' he said. 'Nothing can go wrong, this is all laid on like a military operation.'

With that he got up and said, 'I've got to go, I've got things to do. Will you pick up my suede jumper from the cleaner's?' and he put a £20 note on the mantelpiece. Then he turned to me. 'I've got to ask you for one more favour before I go. Don't go mad,' he said.

'Well, what is it?' I asked.

'Give me a stocking, Princess,' he replied.

'No!' I screamed at him. 'I don't even want you to go and you want me to give you a stocking!'

He gave me a big cuddle and said, 'Please, come on, I will be back before you know it.'

I stormed into the bedroom, opened my stocking drawer and pulled out a black stocking with a red lace top.

'One stocking!' I snapped as I shoved it into his hand.

'Oh Babe, can't I have an ordinary one?' he asked.

'No,' I said, 'that's my little protest.'

He laughed, kissed the stocking and said: 'Okay Princess, this stocking will be lucky for me. I'll wear it. It appeals to me. At least it's different.'

I just held him tight and whispered, 'Be careful.' Then he was gone.

The next morning I went and picked up his cleaning, got a few bits from the corner shop, and went back home to sit and wait. It was 16 December 1980. What a difference a day makes, as the song goes.

I made coffee and sat down to watch the news. The lead story was about a major armed robbery that the police had foiled. Everybody had been arrested. I turned off the TV. I knew it was Ronnie. December, bloody December! Once again that month had changed my life. I sat down and sobbed my heart out.

In the early evening Paul Pemberton, Ronnie's nephew, called at the flat. They had been due to meet during the day, but Ron had not arrived and after seeing the TV news Paul was putting two and two together. We both realised that Ronnie would never reveal my existence to the police, so Paul promised to visit Ronnie's wife Renee to find out what was happening. He telephoned later to confirm that Ronnie had been arrested.

Griff called round and promised to find out more information for me. Suddenly I was an outsider. I felt bereaved but, unlike when Micky was killed, all the activity was at Ronnie's home and his wife was the centre of attention.

The following day I was in my kitchen when a disgusting, filthy old tramp shuffled up and knocked on the window. When I opened the door, I was astonished to find that the 'tramp' was actually one of Ronnie's friends in disguise. He had seen the news stories but was initially doubtful about Ronnie's involvement because, as he said, the secret of Ronnie's success was that he never worked with more than two others, and this had been a major gang heist.

Barely concealed beneath the tramp's clothing I could see that the man was carrying a gun. He had been due to carry out a robbery that day with Ronnie – just the two of them – arriving independently and leaving separately. At the appointed time he turned up at the scene of the intended crime, but had to abandon it when Ronnie failed to show up.

'Linda, I am shocked,' he said. 'I can't believe Ron would go on a robbery with six other people. He said he didn't really need money and in any case today we were going on this really sweet bit of work that would have given us £70,000 to £80,000 each.' With that he kissed me on the cheek and left, promising to help in any way he could.

I was just numbed to think that Ronnie had been planning a second armed robbery the very next day and had kept this from me as well.

Over the next few days I was isolated from events as Ronnie's family were the only ones who could safely visit him and attend the magistrates court hearings. Then one day the phone rang and it was Nicky, a young girl who had come with us on the holiday to Corfu. Her boyfriend Kevin had also been arrested and charged and she was able to visit him in Brixton Prison every day. Ronnie had sent a message through Kevin to say that he was sorry. He loved me more than anything else in the world and was going crazy not being able to see me. He promised to arrange through Nicky a safe time for me to visit.

A couple of days before Christmas Nicky rang with the message that I was to go on New Year's Day and take Griff along with me.

When the time for the visit came, I stood in the queue outside the Brixton Prison gates, contemplating the sad start to the new year and praying that things would get better.

We were soon inside that dismal, dirty place and taken to the top security room which contained just three tables with the chairs screwed to the floor, guarded by a couple of prison officers. When Ronnie walked in I leaned across the board that separated us and just held him in my arms. As we sat down there was a tear trickling down his face. He wiped it away with the back of his hand and said it must have been an eyelash that got into his eye by accident.

Griff was so choked. 'You didn't really want to see me Ronnie, I'll wait outside,' he said.

'Thanks, Griff,' said Ronnie. 'It's true, it's my Princess I wanted to see. I just didn't want her travelling here all by herself. I'll see you next time.'

They shook hands and Griff left, wishing Ronnie good luck.

The rest of the visit was immersed in a blur of tears for me as he told me the story of his capture.

The robbery was a raid on a Brinks Mat security van in south London and had proved so complicated to organise that the gang had called Ronnie in at the last minute as an extra pair of hands.

Apparently, one member of the robbery gang had been arrested over another matter and, if convicted, was facing a jail term of about three years. It was one of those things, a hazard of the job. If you can't do the time don't do the crime. This man, however, had done a deal with the police by telling them, in return for his freedom, about the robbery which was due to take place. He had given the police the time and place and the names of all the gang members except for Ronnie, whose involvement he had been unaware of in advance.

The plan was for this police informer to take part in the robbery so as not to arouse the suspicions of the other robbers. He would be set free as soon as the gang were rounded up.

In the event the robbery was successful and the team seized £800,000 before the police moved in – about fifty of them, mostly armed, according to Ronnie. He, being a fitness fanatic, ran away and was the only one to make his escape. Typically, though, he went back to see if he could help any of his mates.

Ironically it was the police informer he found lying on the ground and moved in to aid his escape, only to find himself looking down the barrel of a policeman's gun. Soon he was lying face down in the roadway with his hands cuffed behind his back, alongside five other members of the gang. As they lay there, they heard a detective call the informer's name. 'Okay mate, go on, go,' they heard him shout. Ronnie watched helplessly as the grass ran away and bitterly swore vengeance on the traitor.

'I promise I will kill him,' he told me. 'It is bad enough that he led us into a trap that got us arrested, but he took us all there knowing the police would be armed and not knowing if any of us would be killed.'

I just continued to sob, but Ronnie cuddled me and said, 'Listen, Sweetheart, all is not lost. Scatts and I have something up our sleeve. I can't tell you at the moment but I will soon be home.'

The only other two members of the gang I knew were Scatts Tobin and Kevin Brown.

On the drive home it was obvious that Griff was ill. By the time we got to Bethnal Green he was grey and blood was pouring out of his mouth. His ulcer had burst over the shock at seeing Ronnie because they had been like brothers since they were teenagers. We called the ambulance and I was once again in tears because I thought he was dying, but he refused to go to the hospital for treatment until he had spoken to me in private. When the ambulancemen left the room he said: 'Linda, I will go to hospital, but only if you swear to me on Ronnie's life that you won't let them keep me in.'

After I had given my word, he was taken off in an ambulance and his wife Kathy and I followed in my car. At the hospital, naturally, they insisted on keeping him in. Kathy told him not to make a fuss, just to stay.

Although he was suffering and looked awful, Griff looked at me and said, 'You promised me you wouldn't let them keep me. You took an oath on Ron's life.'

Kathy was having none of it and stormed out of the hospital, on her way home.

Griff was too weak to walk so, in desperation, I tore down the corridors until I found an unattended wheelchair. Just as I loaded him in it, a porter arrived to move him. I ran off down the passageway, pushing the wheelchair, with the porter panting after me and protesting that I couldn't remove an admitted patient.

When we reached the hospital entrance I abandoned the chair, put Griff's arms around my neck and physically dragged him to my car. I took him home, much to the annoyance of Kathy, and when I finally arrived at my flat I collapsed exhausted, thinking 'Bloody hell, what a year . . . and we're still only on the first day!!!'

6

SOLDIER, SOLDIER

As those first few weeks of 1981 unfolded it became painfully obvious that my life was changing. I had come down to earth with a bump. Gone was the £100 put on my mantelpiece every Friday night. I had no choice; I went and signed on the dole. I felt utterly degraded.

On the outside I appeared to have everything – a flat full of beautiful furniture, designer clothes, furs, jewellery, a nice car – but there was no money coming in. Ronnie had spoiled me so much, I was finding it hard to manage.

I could only visit Ronnie once a fortnight and I hated it. I didn't go out, just sat in every night. Ronnie had been so preoccupied with sorting out his predicament and making arrangements for his family that I didn't want to bother him with my woes. Soon, however, he was worrying about me too. He sent a message to Brian

Thorogood and instructed him to accompany me on a visit. As I mentioned, Brian and I had not hit it off too well in our earlier encounters, and it was clear that Brian was reluctant, but he chatted quite warmly in the car on the way to Brixton and was obviously pleased to see Ronnie whom he embraced with genuine affection.

Ronnie explained my financial difficulties and asked Brian to arrange for me to be paid from the funds of his own company, but Brian said that I could be paid from his company. He promised to arrange a weekly payout, plus an immediate £250 to cover my telephone and gas bills.

He had been told to look after me and that's exactly what he did. It is the done thing in the underworld when a big fish goes on a laydown – their families are taken care of. The big fish still calls the tune from behind bars.

Brian was originally a soldier, a Royal Fusilier, and there was still a lot of the military man about him – loyalty, a willingness to obey orders and, as I was to learn later, meticulous planning when it came to carrying out a criminal operation like armed robbery.

Afterwards, when we got to my flat, I made Brian a cup of tea and a couple of sandwiches before he went back to work. He promised to call on the Friday with my weekly payment. As he left he turned and said: 'Bye for now, see you Friday, Sid.'

'My name's not Sid,' I retorted. He laughed.

'You're not a princess either, but it doesn't stop Ronnie calling you Princess,' he said.

'Well, I can understand him calling me Princess, but why Sid?' I asked.

'You look like a Sid to me,' he replied, and from that day on I was always Sid to Brian.

Some months later Ronnie again called for Brian to accompany me on a visit because he needed to talk business with him. After the business had been sorted out, Brian said: 'I'll tell you what Ron, I could do with changing places with you for a week. I am having murders at home at the moment. The rest would do me good. It's all over tomorrow night. The firm's got a dinner laid on for a couple of important clients and my wife doesn't want to go.'

'Take my Princess instead,' said Ronnie. 'That will impress them, wondering how you got somebody so good-looking and smart.'

'I never thought of that,' said Brian. 'Would you like to go, Sid?'

I said I would be delighted, so long as Ronnie didn't mind.

Ronnie said: 'Go. It will do you good. It's ages since you've been out, and besides, he thinks you're a fella, calling you Sid, so that's no problem.'

We all laughed.

The following day I had my hair done and dressed up in black velvet trousers, little black pumps with gemstones on them and a long-sleeved sequinned top. When Brian knocked on the door he simply said, 'Sid. You look beautiful.' To which I replied, 'Thank you, kind Sir.'

When I was introduced to the guests of honour as 'Sid' the lady exclaimed, 'What a beautiful name. Were you named after Cyd Charisse?'

'I don't think so,' I said, stifling a giggle.

During the evening Brian's partner mentioned that he needed to take on two people to work in the warehouse. Brian suggested that I take the job and, although his partner said it was dirty work more suited to men, he agreed to let me talk it over with my sister-in-law Maureen to see if we both wanted the job.

We had a lovely time and I really enjoyed myself. It was great to be happy and laughing once again.

At the end of the evening Brian took me home and came in for a coffee. I switched on the table lamp, put on an old Nat King Cole album that Micky had kept in prison, and sat on the settee facing him.

He said, 'I can see why Ronnie loves you, Sid. You are a beautiful woman.'

I laughed and said, 'You're quite tasty yourself. I like men in suits.'

'It's like sitting in a club. This music and soft lights. Would you like to dance?' he asked, getting to his feet.

He held me close and we danced really slowly without saying a word until the album finished playing. Then he said, curtly, 'Thanks. I enjoyed that. I am going now.' With that he kissed me on the cheek and left abruptly.

Maureen leapt at the chance of a job in the warehouse, so we both agreed to give it a try.

Brian had promised to pick us up each morning and bring us home each night, but when I opened the door to him the first day he was clearly taken aback to see me wearing no make-up or jewellery and dressed in jeans, trainers and a T-shirt. 'I hardly recognised you, Sid,' he said. 'I only ever think of you looking like you've just stepped out of Harrods' window.'

'You're making me embarrassed,' I told him.

'Sorry,' he said, 'I just never imagined you possessed a pair of jeans, that's all.'

Maureen and I were put to the test in the first few weeks by the owner who really wanted a couple of men to work in his warehouse. He went out of his way to give us the dirtiest and toughest jobs, in an attempt to break our spirits, but we both needed the work and we were determined not to be beaten. The work involved plenty of heavy lifting, but, no matter what was thrown at us, we bent our backs and set about proving that we were as good as the men. Eventually we won the admiration and support of all the male staff in the company and became accepted as part of the team.

The worst job we had to do was to bleach a whole lorry load of broomsticks. Oh, how the mighty had fallen. We wore black dustbin liners over our clothes, face masks and industrial rubber gloves.

Ronnie was pleased that I was working and earning good money, and I was relieved that he didn't ask what the work entailed, but one day during a prison visit he held my hands in his and looked at me with a shocked expression.

'What's happened to your nails and the skin of your hands, Princess?' he asked.

When I told him the kind of work I was doing he went raving mad. 'I am not having you working like a navvy,' he yelled. 'I thought you were working in the offices.'

He soon got Brian to have an office job invented for me, and Maureen, who was a barmaid, went back to bar work. We had all seen the job as a temporary move anyway, because Ronnie was totally confident that he would be home free as soon as his trial came up at the Old Bailey.

When I asked Ron why he was so confident, he confided that he and a friend were planning to have the jury bribed to bring in Not Guilty verdicts for himself, Scatts Tobin, and Kevin Brown. Ronnie was going to get his own people to arrange the bribery. I asked what would happen to the other three defendants and Ronnie said, 'It is sad, but we just don't think a jury would stand it for all six people.'

The week before the trial, he told me that he was arranging to pay his friend's people the bribe money. He was not going to worry about using his own people as the jury would be frightened off if they were approached by more than one group.

Ronnie had also developed an extremely good defence for why he was at the scene of the robbery. After all, his name had not been on the list given to the police, and their informer was not going to be giving evidence because the police were denying his existence and declaring that the six people arrested were the only ones involved.

The robbery had taken place outside a south London school during the children's lunchbreak. There had been a mobile hamburger van parked there at the time. As luck would have it, the man working in the van was a person who had been involved in a long-running feud with Ronnie's nephew Paul Pemberton. So Ronnie's alibi was that he had gone to confront the hamburger seller and warn him to stay away from his nephew. When he saw a group of men fighting, he instinctively went to the aid of the one he thought was getting the worst of it.

I felt so much better hearing all this. I was convinced that Ronnie's promises would be fulfilled and I would soon have him home.

It wasn't possible for me to attend the trial because Ronnie's family were there to support him almost every day. We arranged for Kevin's girlfriend Nicky to bring me up to date on the day's events each evening.

It was a long trial because all six men were offering separate alibis. The police produced a video they had filmed of the robbery taking place, but you could not identify Ronnie in it because he was wearing my black stocking over his head. I was glad that he'd taken it from me after all.

About four weeks into the trial Nicky received a message that Ronnie's family would not be attending the Old Bailey the following day, so I arranged to go with her. As it was I did not pay any attention to what was going on because Ronnie and I spent the entire day gazing lovingly at each other, smiling and blowing kisses – me from the public gallery and him from the dock. The only thing I noticed was my black silk stocking with the red lace top lying on the exhibits table.

Eventually it came time for the jury to return their verdicts and I was relieved it was all over. Ronnie had paid his share of the bribe money to his friend so his Not Guilty verdict was a mere formality – or so I thought. To my astonishment and horror Kevin was acquitted, no verdict was returned for Scatts and he got a retrial, but Ronnie and the others were all found Guilty. Ronnie was sentenced to sixteen years. I was numb with disbelief. Clearly the jury hadn't been got at after all.

It was the first time in living memory that an Old Bailey trial ended on a Saturday evening. The press reported that the jury had been given a 24-hour armed guard throughout and armed uniformed police and detectives guarded the court. After the sentences were handed down, relatives and friends in the public gallery hurled a torrent of abuse and threats at the judge, the jury and the police. Loud applause and cheering greeted the acquittal of Kevin Brown.

The prosecution had told the court that an armed gang staged an attack on a 7½-ton Brinks Mat security van carrying £811,000 outside Kingsdale Comprehensive School in Dulwich. A skip lorry pulled out in front of the van, then the jib of a hijacked crane rammed through the back door and a stolen car pulled up alongside, sandwiching the van.

However, armed detectives from the Flying Squad and Robbery Squad were lying in wait to catch the gang red-handed after a tip-off from one of the gang members referred to in court as Mr X. A video-recording of the ambush was made and the jury saw detectives pouncing on the gang. After a brief flurry of gunshots, six men were arrested while Mr X escaped. He did not go to court to give evidence. It was alleged that he had colluded with Scotland Yard detectives to set up the robbery to try to frame one of the gang members.

During the trial, prison officers uncovered a determined escape plan involving some of the gang. A hacksaw blade was found on one of them and a search showed that bars in a multiple cell in the Old Bailey had been practically sawn through.

After the trial, as one man in the public gallery shouted to jury members: 'Let's hope you sleep well, the lot of you', the Judge told the jury that their armed protection would continue. Excusing them from jury service for ten years, he said they were unlikely to be in danger once they had returned their verdicts.

Linda takes up the story again:

My first visit to Ronnie after that was very emotional. I asked him what had gone wrong with his plan for freedom.

'As if it's not bad enough that slag grassing us up,' he said, 'now my mate has had me over too. It is obvious he didn't get to the jury.' I know now why he was so insistent that his people did the sting and not mine. He has had me well and truly over, but he will pay. I swear I will kill him for what he has done to me.'

I said: 'I know it's terrible but that's two people you want to kill now. Hatred will eat you up.'

'No, Princess,' he replied, 'hatred will carry me through this sentence and make me strong. Revenge is sweet and everyone who knows me knows I don't make idle threats.'

He told me that he would appeal against his sentence.

'But I'm telling you here and now that I won't get anywhere,' he said. 'Sixteen years I have been given. That's ten years and eight months with remission and I have no illusions. I won't be home until I have served at least ten years, Princess.'

I couldn't imagine what he was going to say next. I was still reeling from the shock of his lengthy sentence. Then he leaned forward, took both of my hands in his, and looked deep into my eyes.

'I love you, Princess,' he said, 'but I am a realist. You are beautiful and free with no ties and I am locked up for a long time. You aren't my wife, not even my common-law wife. If at the end of this ten-year nightmare you are standing outside those gates waiting for me, that is all I can ask. I don't expect you to stay faithful and I expect you will have affairs. I don't mind. Just don't flaunt it.' Be there for me every visiting day. Look pretty for me.'

He told me to think about it: 'I know I've got no right to ask it of you . . .'

I thought he had every right. I promised without hesitation that I would wait for him. No lies. I couldn't promise I wouldn't have boyfriends while he was away, but I wouldn't mug him off. Later I discovered that it was the norm for gangsters' women to have boyfriends while their old man was away, but as soon as the husband came out of prison the boyfriend had to disappear. It was the unspoken rule. As long as you didn't mug them off, it was okay.

Ronnie told me that as he was a Category A prisoner I would have to be vetted before I was allowed to visit him. He said I was to call myself his common-law wife and give my name as Miss Welford – my maiden name – because he didn't think the prison authorities would allow any visits from Linda Calvey, the widow of an armed robber shot dead by the police in controversial circumstances.

When it came time for my next visit I decided to do something that would put his mind at rest and show that I was determined to be there for him at the end of the day. I hit on the idea of a tattoo, because they are permanent, and had 'True Love Ronnie Cook' put at the top of my left leg. I was too vain to have anything on my arms or shoulders which might show.

When I walked into the visiting room I said to Ronnie, 'I have a surprise for you,' and lifted my skirt to reveal the tattoo. 'That's just to prove that no matter what happens in between, at the end of the day there is no doubt that you and I are meant to be together,' I said.

Ronnie was thrilled.

As the next Christmas approached I went shopping with Maureen and saw a beautiful black crêpe dress with jet beads around the collar. It was £185. I decided to buy it for myself as I would not be getting anything special for Christmas.

On the way to work in the car the next day, I casually told Brian about the dress and that I intended to buy it the following Saturday. Imagine my surprise the following Friday when Brian slipped me £300 as he dropped me off at home.

'Buy yourself that dress and spend the change on a couple of presents from me for the kids,' he said. 'I wanted to get you something and didn't know what, so this has solved the problem.'

Then he added: 'Listen Sid, don't you buy me a present. There's nothing I need and I would only get murders at home if I took anything indoors anyway.'

So I agreed to compromise and take him out for a meal.

When I bought the dress the following day Maureen grinned at me and said: 'I don't know how you do it. You always get blokes wanting to spend money on you.'

'Brian isn't my bloke. He's just a friend,' I chuckled.

A week later I took Brian out for a meal at an Italian restaurant in Greenwich near the Cutty Sark. It was a lovely evening. Brian looked very smart in a suit and tie. I wore a dark purple suit. We chatted and joked all evening and when Brian tried to pay the bill, protesting that he'd never let a woman pay for him before, I told him it was my Christmas treat for him and he'd just have to break the habit of a lifetime. Eventually he agreed, on condition that I let him return the compliment on another occasion.

Back at my flat for coffee, we went through the same routine we'd shared after the firm's dinner while Ronnie was on remand. We held each other close and danced slowly and romantically until the music stopped. Then he kissed me on the cheek and left abruptly.

The next day Maureen telephoned.

'Well?' she asked.

'Well, what? I replied.

'Don't mess about,' she said. 'You went out for a romantic meal together, yes?'

'Yes.'

'You brought him home with you, yes?'

'Yes.'

'Well, did you do the dirty deed?'

'No Maureen,' I said. 'He doesn't fancy me. All he did was have a dance and went home.'

That was too much for her.

'Don't tell me you've lost your touch,' she spluttered.

A couple of days before Christmas I received a bouquet of a dozen red and a dozen pink roses from Ronnie with an envelope containing £500 and a note saying: 'Sorry we are apart. Buy a present for yourself and the kids.'

I bought a pair of boots and a matching handbag and spent the rest on the children. Christmas and New Year were a bit lonely, being among the family but being the only one without a partner.

In the first week of the New Year Brian took me out to repay me for the meal I had bought him. We went to an Italian restaurant in Hornchurch and this time I decided he wasn't going to go home after a dance. I wore a very sexy tight black lace dress, an extra dash of perfume, and very high black court shoes with diamanté ankle straps. I knew he was mine that night. All evening I just fluttered my eyelashes at him and listened intently to every word he had to say.

When we got back to my flat once again I made the coffee, put the music on sweet and low and said: 'Well, where's my dance? It's traditional. You know that.'

We did not say a word as we danced. I slipped my hands under his jacket and removed it. I smiled at him and began to loosen his tie. Suddenly, with a mild curse under his breath, he blurted out, 'I can't hold out any longer.' Scooping me up in his arms he carried me into the bedroom.

Afterwards, as he was leaving, I said, 'And I didn't think you fancied me.'

'You're crazy,' he replied. 'I've wanted you since that first night I took you out, but Ronnie is my friend and I have had to wrestle with my conscience over this.'

'I told you the deal I have with Ronnie,' I said. 'I love him and will be with him at the end of the day, but he has told me he wouldn't expect from me what he couldn't do himself. If you want to see me under those circumstances, I would like it very much. What do you say?'

'Sid, I couldn't say no,' he said. 'I can see why Ronnie loves you. You're not like any woman I have ever met.'

With that he left, but he was back the next morning for a coffee, and when he learned that I planned a shopping spree he gave me £100 and told me that if I found something I liked that was a bit more expensive he would add the difference.

I didn't need a second invitation and was soon trotting into my favourite fur shop with Maureen in tow. A red fox three-quarter length jacket took my fancy. It cost £700 and the little matching fur hat which I decided to add was £70. I put down Brian's £100 as a deposit and Maureen asked: 'How do you know that he will pay for it?'

The lady in the shop who had sold me a number of furs paid for by Ronnie said: 'Oh her boyfriend lets her have anything she wants.'

'Well, he's in prison, this isn't her boyfriend,' retorted Maureen.

'I know that, but I'm sure he'll think I'm worth it,' I said.

When Brian turned up after work that evening, he refused to sit in the lounge because his clothes were dirty. Instead he sat on the fridge in the kitchen while I made him a cup of coffee. He asked what I had bought and I told him a hat and a coat, but it did cost a little bit more than he had given me. I stood his coffee on the fridge next to him and casually handed him the receipt. I turned around to pick up my own coffee, heard a bang, looked back, and Brian had fallen off the fridge.

'What happened?' I laughed.

'I read this receipt, that's what happened,' he said. 'When you said a hat and a coat I thought you'd bought a raincoat or something like that.'

I looked at him with a sorrowful expression and asked innocently: 'Have I spent too much money then?'

'No. It's not your fault,' he said. 'You're used to being spoiled. Ronnie's a hard act to follow.'

'Does that mean I can't have it? I said, still looking at him with sad eyes. He put his arms around me and said, 'Of course you can have it. You deserve it, Sid.'

The next time I saw Ronnie he said he was worrying about me and wanted me to have more security, so he had smuggled a note out of prison to his business partner instructing him to put half the shares of his company into my name. That way, he said, I would get all the benefits like having certain bills paid and a company car with tax, insurance and petrol all paid for by the firm.

His partner was very strongly opposed to the idea. He refused to put the shares in my name but agreed to give me all the perks. I didn't mind about not having a share in the company but told Ronnie that his partner had put the shares in my name – I didn't want him adding another enemy to his list of revenge targets. I was given a blue Datsun coupé as my company car, so I sold my own car and cancelled my insurance.

By this time Brian and I were an item. The relationship with his wife had totally broken down and they agreed to part, splitting the proceeds from the sale of their house in half. He moved in with some friends and I went straight to the prison and told Ron. He was very relaxed about it. As far as he was concerned, we had a deal and as long as I stuck to my side of the bargain and didn't mug him off, things would be all right.

When it came to my birthday that year the usual huge bouquet of red roses arrived from Ronnie with a parcel attached to it. Inside was a huge sparkler – a ring consisting of an oval ruby surrounded by thirty-six diamonds.

Brian also sent me flowers and announced that he would take me out that evening. I bought myself a new dress and hoped that he had not bought me a ring for my birthday present. When he arrived he was carrying a black dustbin liner. Inside was the most beautiful full-length fox fur coat. He had guessed that Ronnie would send me jewellery and had gone for the other thing he knew I adored. I put it on immediately and wore it to go out for my celebration meal.

Eventually I persuaded Brian to invest the money from the sale of his family home in another property. He wanted to move out of the East End but didn't want to move to Grays because he didn't want to live too close to the business. He was not at all interested in house hunting, so I spent weeks and months trailing around estate agents and viewing properties.

Finally, I found a sweet little terraced house in a quiet tree-lined road in Hornchurch with a huge garden which backed on to a stream and a large park. I set to work with a builder and we turned it into country-cottage style with wooden beams, an open fireplace and an oak fitted kitchen.

When Brian took over the house we began to spend every weekend there and soon made firm friends with the neighbours. My son Neil, who was nine years old, also made friends and began to beg me to move to Hornchurch permanently. My brother Tony and his girlfriend were living in my flat at weekends because it was empty, but my daughter Melanie spent the time with my mother because she wasn't so keen on Hornchurch.

One day Brian said: 'Look Linda, you are happy in that little house and Neil loves it. I like being here at weekends, but it doesn't bother me one way or the other if I am here or in London. I am going to give you this house as a present. I know you will let me be here whenever I want. Neil can go to school here and you are a lot nearer to the firm. I'm sure Mel would be okay here too.'

I looked at him and said: 'What did you say?' He began to repeat his proposal but I stopped him. 'You called me Linda,' I said.

'Well, that's your name and I've decided not to call you Sid anymore,' he said.

I argued that Linda didn't sound right after being called Sid for so long, but he came back to the point. 'I want to give you this house. No strings attached. What do you say?' he insisted.

'You know that I intend to end up with Ronnie, and it is a very big present, but if you are sure then I would love the house,' I said.

Melanie stayed on at my mother's until she was sure about the move and Tony and his girlfriend stayed in my flat until I was settled in Hornchurch.

I told Ronnie about the move and gave him the new address. He was happy that I was moving out of London and said he had intended to do that for me when he came out of prison anyway.

Brian stopped calling me Linda, but never called me Sid again. He confessed that when he first saw me I was wearing so much jewellery he was reminded of a rude East End nickname given to Jews – 'Sid the Yid'. Now he thought the name too disrespectful for his lover, so from then on he called me 'Sunshine'.

7

OVER THE PAVEMENT

I had been given some presents in my time, but never anything as valuable or generous as a house. After Brian's lovely gesture in handing me ownership of our little home in Hornchurch – which sold very quickly – I set about looking for a larger property of my own.

I soon found a beautiful mock-Tudor house nearby in Harold Wood. It had been carefully looked after and decorated to a high standard with leaded-light windows, marble fireplaces, immaculate carpets and up-market fitted curtains in every room. The master bedroom was the most luxurious I had ever seen – absolute five-star quality – it could have come straight from the TV series *Dynasty*.

So we moved in together and I told Ron that I'd bought my own house, but I omitted to tell him that it was a present from Brian who was living there with me. For a while we enjoyed an idyllic existence. My kids adored the house and were doing very well at their local schools.

One day Brian went out very early in the morning and came back with a mate of his I had never seen before and said: 'Do us a favour, love. Cook us a couple of breakfasts while I just nip to the garage up the road. I won't be ten minutes.'

Well, his mate and I waited for over three hours and he didn't come back. His friend walked up to the garage and couldn't see Brian, so eventually I gave him a lift into London. Later on I discovered that Brian had been pounced on by the Flying Squad while he chatted to a friend outside the garage. They'd accused him of planning to rob the till, and wouldn't listen when he told them that only a fool would attempt a robbery so early in the day, when the takings would be too small to be bothered with. They searched his bag and found a knife, so they arrested him for possession of an offensive weapon.

Brian never told me the truth of that episode, but looking back I expect he was actually casing the joint with a view to robbing it, possibly along with his mysterious breakfast friend, when the tills were actually full at the end of the day, The police had obviously been tipped-off in advance.

Anyway, when he got to court he pleaded guilty to possession of the knife, and to his astonishment was sentenced to a year. He ended up in High Point Prison, so once again I was on my own with Neil and Melanie. Brian's business had gone into liquidation, so Ron stepped in again and found me a job with another company in which he owned shares. However, the money wasn't so good and I joined my mum's café where I worked with my sisters. It was a laugh being together, running a sort of family business.

While Brian was away I was introduced to Billy Blundell, a very wealthy Essex businessman.

When we met he said: 'I know who you are because I saw your television programme.' He was referring to a discussion programme presented by John Stapleton about the death of my Micky. 'Did you see mine?' he asked, because *World in Action* had done a programme on him and his brother Eddie, accusing them unjustly of involvement in protection rackets. 'How could they make such ridiculous accusations against us?' he asked. I had to admit that I had missed his moment of TV counter-stardom, but I later saw the tape at his house and we had a good laugh about it.

Pretty soon Billy and I had become really close friends. We used to go out together for meals and drinks and I became a frequent visitor to his beautiful farm in Essex. I also accompanied him to some really good parties and he introduced me to some very interesting people. He was a great character and commanded respect wherever he was. He was a really nice man and he used to say that he loved coming round to my house because it was a haven where he could get away from it all. He arranged to have the front drive tarmacked for me and an ornamental pond put in.

Billy wasn't very tall and his brother Eddie was well over six-foot. He used to make me laugh by saying, 'Only our mother can tell us apart,' when there was about eighteen inches between them in height.

I've always got on well with men and while Brian was away all my male friends used to come round regularly. The neighbours got a bit snooty because they couldn't understand how a young woman with two kids could always have really nice cars like Jaguars and Mercedes parked in front of her house. The constant appearance of Billy's Rolls-Royce was too much for some of them.

While Brian was in prison he decided that if he was going to be arrested and jailed for something as stupid as carrying a knife, he wasn't going to go back to work. He was going to do a few armed robberies to make enough money to retire altogether. His reasoning was that if he was going to commit crime he was determined to do something worth being arrested for.

So, when he came home after a year, he began to recruit a team of people with the different skills you need as a robbery gang and started to supplement his meagre income by going back out on armed post office and security van robberies. I knew what he was doing and sometimes I would go with him to 'case' the post offices and to time the security vans making their deliveries. I had given up my job to spend more time with him and we were enjoying the good life. I had a nice car, I was able to buy nice clothes again and treat my children to all the good things. It was great.

It came round to 1985 and Brian had looked at a couple of suitable targets with the other members of his gang. There were two early in that year. First we looked at a post office in Gidea Park. Then, after it was robbed and Brian got the money, he decided to rob the post office security van which made a regular visit to the post office in Globe Road, Plaistow – the same road where my flat was. We needed to keep surveillance so that we could note the precise timings of the van's arrival and departure and how that varied from day to day.

By this time we had recruited Brian Croly, who was the neighbour over the road from the first house we had bought in Hornchurch. We had become good friends with him and his wife and he'd been given the job of keeping a watch on the post offices that were going to be robbed. Normally, he and I would alternate in walking past the target or hanging about keeping watch so that anyone keeping an eye open wouldn't be suspicious about seeing the same person every day.

My brother Tony and his new wife were living in my flat. They were entirely honest and law-abiding and would not have entertained us having anything to do with armed robberies if they had known.

This time the surveillance strategy relied on a degree of subterfuge involving Tony and Sandra who had to be kept in the dark about what was going on. Whenever we knew roughly that the security van was due at the post office Brian and I, along with another member of the team Carl Gibney, would pop in on my brother and his wife for a cup of tea. Throughout each of these apparently casual social encounters one of us would stand by the window which gave a clear view of the post office. Whoever was on this makeshift sentry duty would make an excuse to pop out to buy cigarettes or a newspaper whenever they saw the van pulling up, and Tony and Sandra were none the wiser.

When it was my turn I also used to use a launderette opposite the post office as my lookout base, but what none of us knew was that we were all under police surveillance ourselves.

When everything was ready and Brian had decided on the date of the attack, we realised that we would need to use my flat as our operational headquarters.

Tony and Sandra were in the habit of staying up until the early hours of the morning and lying in bed the next day until late. As luck would have it, the robbery was due to take place first thing in the morning, so I asked my brother's permission to pop in. I made up a story about Brian having to get to an early meeting in London and promised to let myself in with my own key so as not to disturb them.

When Brian, Carl and I arrived, sure enough Tony and Sandra were sound asleep in bed so we were able to get the camouflage gear and balaclavas on and load and check the weapons without being disturbed. Carl and Brian had already parked the getaway cars – you always have a second car a few streets away, usually parked at the end of a pedestrian alleyway, so that you can make a switch to throw pursuers off the scent and prevent anyone who might be chasing in a car from cutting off your escape route. So everything was set.

Then as Brian and Carl went down to hold the van up, they were surrounded by armed police, thrown to the ground and arrested. The police came racing up to my flat and began beating on the door, which woke up Tony and Sandra. I answered the door and both Tony and I were thrown on the floor with guns pointed at our heads. I swear the fattest man in the squad was the one who jumped on me. He nearly squashed the life out of me and pointed the gun right at my eye. I remember looking straight up the barrel.

Brian and Carl were charged with robbery and conspiracy to rob. Tony, Sandra and I were also charged with conspiracy to rob. Brian felt terrible about it because not only did he not want me involved, but also he knew that Tony and Sandra were entirely innocent. He offered a deal to the police. He told them that I needed to be with my children and promised to admit to a number of robberies he had committed, in return for the three of us being given bail.

When it came to our first appearance in court, the head of the Robbery Squad kept his side of the bargain and we were given unconditional bail – a situation which remained unchanged for more than a year until our trial.

Brian was sent to Brixton Prison as a Category A prisoner. I visited him most days and, because he was on remand, I was allowed to take him home-cooked meals.

One day, Brian told me about this bloke he had met in there called Danny Reece. He was young and hotheaded but kind to Brian and I was soon persuaded to cook meals for him too. When I met him I instinctively liked him. He was a fitness fanatic, big, strong and quite disconcertingly good-looking.

His only visitor was his mum who lived at Stratford in the East End. It was difficult for her to get to and from Brixton by public transport because she had fallen and broken her arm, so I volunteered to give her a lift whenever I was visiting. She was a lovely lady who doted on Danny. He was obviously the favourite of all her children. She was worried about the fact that her son appeared to have given up hope and no longer cared what happened to him. So, in an effort to cheer him up, I used to get him out of his cell and up to the visitors' room from time to time when his mother wasn't there. He didn't say much. He just sat and studied the faces of the people in the room and rarely spoke.

Over the fifteen months until my trial I got to know Danny quite well. Later he was to tell me what an impression I had made on him when he first saw me. I was wearing a full-length fur coat because I always felt it was important to dress up for prison visits, so that no one could look down on me or the prisoners I was visiting. On this particular day, Danny recalled, I strolled into the tiny Cat A visitors' room, took the fur coat from round my shoulders and tossed it at the prison guard with the words 'Hold that, mate!' He was apparently so shocked at my cheek that he caught the coat and held it for me throughout the visit.

I suppose I was a bit flash in those days.

When Danny went to court for his trial, even though I knew he was going to plead Guilty, I went and bought him a little Good Luck card. Many years later he told me it was the only card he'd received which I thought was sad, but it is something very few people ever think of. When Brian and I went to court nobody sent us cards. I didn't even think of sending Brian or Carl, my co-defendants, a card. When Danny got sentenced to thirteen years I was very sad and I wrote to him expressing my sorrow and asked him to write to me.

At this stage I had an almost full-time, six-days-a-week job as a prison visitor and provider of meals, calling at Brixton to see Brian, at Coldingley to see Carl Gibney and at Gartree to see Ronnie.

About six months before all this happened, Terry O'Leary, my very first boyfriend who had given me the black eye, came back into my life. He went to see one of my brothers and managed to track me down for old time's sake. He turned up at the Harold Wood house one Saturday morning when I was out having my hair done and told Brian who he was. Brian lent him his car to collect me from the hairdresser's as a surprise, which was lovely, and after that we all became firm friends. So, when Brian was arrested and sent to Brixton, Terry volunteered to come with me once a week, every Tuesday, for visits.

One day, however, he didn't turn up to give me my lift, which was entirely uncharacteristic of him. He'd never been in trouble with the police or been in prison so I had no inkling of what was to come. I apologised to Brian for missing the visit and we both speculated as to what might have happened. Two days later Brian said to me: 'I've found out why Terry didn't collect you on Tuesday. He's in here and I think he's charged with murder.'

I was dumbstruck.

'Stop it, I don't believe you,' I said, but Brian insisted.

'I couldn't believe it either,' he said, 'but when I bumped into him unexpectedly in the corridor I asked him why on earth he was in prison and he said: 'I've killed someone.''

Well, Terry's incarceration meant that I immediately had to add yet another inmate to my already overcrowded programme of prison visits. When I got to see him for the first time, he told me that he'd heard his wife had been having an affair with someone, and her lover's friends had taunted and humiliated him when he was drinking on his own in the pub one night. Terry is usually very quiet and laid back, but he wasn't going to stand for that, so he went and got a gun with the intention of shooting his tormentor in the kneecaps to teach him a lesson.

'I got the gun and came back to shoot him,' he told me. 'Honest to God, Lin, I fired at his knees and it went straight through his heart and killed him. I can't believe how it happened. It was a terrible accident. I only meant to hurt him, not to kill him. How could I aim at his legs and hit him in the chest?'

I felt so sorry for him and said: 'I don't know how it could have happened, but you know guns are notoriously difficult to handle and the sights are so often inaccurate. You shouldn't mess with them if you don't know what you're doing.'

Terry was later convicted of manslaughter and sentenced to nine years.

When the time came for our trial I was desperately nervous. I had been to court with Micky numerous times, but it is a different kettle of fish when you are standing in the dock yourself. We appeared at Southwark Crown Court and I pleaded Not Guilty, claiming that I had done what I did under duress. Brian and Carl made statements saying that they had compelled me to play a part in the robbery.

Brian pleaded guilty to twenty-one armed robberies and Carl admitted to something like nine. That left my brother Tony, his wife Sandra and Brian Croly all pleading Not Guilty along with me, so we were still on bail.

As Brian and Carl had pleaded Guilty they were sentenced early on. Brian was given twenty-one years of imprisonment. Carl was given fourteen. As they left the dock I grinned at Brian and whispered: 'A mere bagatelle!'

When he saw me later he said: 'If I could have reached across and chinned you I would have done. I couldn't believe that I had just got a 21-stretch and you came out with such a flippant remark as that.'

Our trial lasted three weeks and as it went on I became more confident that I would be acquitted. There was certainly no doubt in my mind that my brother and his wife would be found not guilty.

However, the trial had a nasty twist at the end. When the jury came back for the first time, they found Sandra Not Guilty, but they needed more time to deliberate about Tony and me. Tony was delighted because he knew that Sandra was not a strong personality and could not have coped with prison. We were both given a lift because it indicated that the jury were leaning towards our side of the story, but when they came back again they found both Tony and me Guilty. Sandra went hysterical. They'd only been married five minutes and had been due to go on honeymoon the day after we were all arrested. One minute they had a lovely new life together and the next he was going to jail.

I was totally gutted because Tony was innocent of the robbery and didn't deserve to be bracketed with me. I had been involved, but he genuinely knew absolutely nothing about it.

When it came to sentencing, we were very apprehensive because, having given Brian twenty-one years and Carl fourteen, he was clearly a very hard judge. The first one he dealt with was Tony who got nine years. There were gasps of disbelief all round the courtroom and Sandra screamed 'No! no! no!' before collapsing in a dead faint.

Then the judge passed me by and sentenced Brian Croly to three years. By this time I was wondering whether or not I would be getting the shortest sentence, having been left until last, but when it was me left standing alone in the dock the judge really launched a verbal attack on me.

I was so shocked that his words have remained with me. As I recall it his remarks were along the lines of: 'I am convinced that the part you played in this crime was far greater than anyone in this court, including the police, has suggested. Far from acting under duress – a small cog in the robbery machine as has been suggested – I believe you were the machine itself.'

I stood there open-mouthed. I thought: 'What is he saying?'

'If I could I would have given you twenty-one years today, the same as your co-defendant Thorogood,' said the judge. 'But it would be a pointless gesture because you would have it reduced on appeal. I then considered giving you fourteen years the same as Gibney, or nine years like your brother, but I am going to give you the longest sentence I can with a recommendation that you serve the whole term. You will go to prison for seven years.'

I was stunned. Me? Seven years? Virtually every one of my friends, all men, had been in jail so I was no stranger to visiting prisons, but I had never spent a day behind bars in my life and had no idea what to expect. The realisation slowly dawned on me that I had never met a woman who had ever been in prison. Back in 1986 it was unheard of for women to get long custodial sentences for anything less than murder. Even the female screw who had been sent up to stand with me in the dock gasped when she heard the sentence.

Linda's highly subjective account of the crimes for which she received her first custodial sentence and of the scenes in court that day – 2 July 1986 – leaves out several crucial details and is naturally biased in her favour. The *Daily Telegraph*'s more dispassionate court report, appearing the following day, paints a very different picture. Under the headline 'Ruthless Raiders Jailed' it reads:

> Five people were jailed for a total of 54 years yesterday for their parts in a series of highly organised armed robberies.
>
> Brian Thorogood, a former Royal Fusilier, who carried out a total of 20 robberies, 16 of them using a sawn-off shotgun, was jailed for 21 years, the court was told.
>
> Passing sentence at Southwark Crown Court, Judge Derek Clarkson, said: 'These robberies were carefully planned and organised. They were skilfully, effectively and ruthlessly carried out.'
>
> On one robbery, a young girl nearly lost her eye when a raider blasted her in the face with a shotgun, as she tried to beat off robbers holding a gun to her father's head.
>
> Thorogood, 47, of Squirrels Heath Road, Harold Hill, admitted 20 robberies and was jailed for 21 years.
>
> Carl Gibney, 36, unemployed of Squirrels Heath Road, Harold Hill, admitted five armed robberies, one attempted armed robbery, and having a firearm with intent, and was jailed for 14 years.
>
> Linda Calvey, 38, Thorogood's live-in lover was jailed for

seven years after being found guilty of conspiring to rob post office employees.

Calvey's brother Anthony Welford, 37, a café owner, of Harpley Square, Globe Road, Stepney, was jailed for nine years for the same offence and for handling £70,000 stolen cash. He pleaded guilty to handling three stolen handbags.

Thorogood's neighbour, Brian Croly, 44, a car salesman, of Northumberland Avenue, Hornchurch, Essex, who admitted conspiracy was jailed for three years.

Welford's wife, Sandra, 41, was acquitted of handling £70,000.

8

THE NEW GIRL IN HOLLOWAY

Linda takes up the story of her dramatic day in court and what followed over the next few months as she tried to adjust to her first experience of prison life:

Outside, in the court cell block, Tony was waiting, but he couldn't hear me when I tried to tell him the length of my sentence – it was coming out in a disembodied squeaky little voice. He just cuddled me and wouldn't listen to my apologies for getting him involved. He was determined to look on the bright side and was already planning our appeals.

The female screw wouldn't lock me up in a cell. She invited me to sit in the staff waiting room. There was a big tubby screw sitting knitting in the corner who asked why I was there and not in a cell.

'I couldn't lock her up, she's just got seven years,' said the first screw.

'She couldn't have, she's never spent a day on remand and she's never even been in Holloway,' said the second one.

'I don't know how it's happened, but she's got it.'

The tubby one looked at me with a sympathetic expression.

'Ah, sit down, love,' she said. 'Let's make you a cup of tea.'

That was my first encounter with the British prison system.

For the court appearance I had been wearing a beautiful silk suit with crocodile-skin shoes and matching handbag and all my jewellery. I asked if I could keep my jewellery, but the screws said I would have to give it up along with the handbag.

My solicitor had come down to the cell block to express his shock and dismay and reassure me that my appeal would be launched immediately on the grounds of what he said was the judge's unreasonable severity. I gave him my handbag, with my watch, my jewellery, and all my money in it, to take back up to my family.

My arrival at Holloway Prison was a complete culture shock. It was a major blow to my morale – almost as though someone had punched me in the face. By the time I arrived, it was quite late and the only two other people in the reception area were both nutters. One was hitting her head repeatedly against the wall and the other kept chanting: 'Turn your head, and pray to God' over and over again. I thought, if this is what Holloway is like I will not survive. I will go insane like these two.

The screws were very sympathetic, but the fact that I was unprepared and ignorant of the prison system proved a bit of a problem that first evening. It turned out that, had I known, I could have kept my watch and a few items of jewellery along with my money. I was also allowed three sets of my own clothes, but all I had was the silk suit I stood up in and the high heels, which were definitely not allowed. They gave me a pair of flat plastic sandals to wear and suggested that I wrote to my family to provide two sets of appropriate clothing – jeans or tracksuits. I could then send my silk suit away and get a third set of more practical clothing to replace it.

If you come into prison with nothing, as I had done, you are issued with a few basic necessities. These include a bedroll, a towel, a flannel with HMP stamped on the corner, a bar of soap, a sachet of shampoo, a cheap comb and a primitive toothbrush. You are also given a prison nightie, which is a deeply unattractive article like your Granny used to wear – stiffly starched wincyette with a V-neck, and long sleeves.

The staff suggested that I have a bath before I left the reception area because there was no knowing how long it might be, once I was in the main prison, before I could take my next bath.

Along with my prison issue kit I found a little wrap of tissue paper containing some pale green powder which, on careful inspection, I concluded was Radox bath salts. It didn't look like a large supply so I tipped the lot into my bath before I got in.

Afterwards I said to one of the screws: 'You've given me a toothbrush but I can't clean my teeth because there's no toothpaste.'

'Yes there is,' she said, 'the green powder in the tissue paper – it's tooth powder.'

'Oh dear!' I said. 'I thought it was Radox. I've just bathed in it.'

You can imagine how they laughed. When the laughter had died down they took pity on me and produced a tube of Sainsbury's toothpaste, which had been confiscated from another inmate, as a special present to the foolish new girl. So I began my seven-year sentence with my sole possession being a second-hand tube of toothpaste.

When that rather awkward initiation was over they took me upstairs and locked me in a tiny single cell. I looked out of the window. All I could see was a big tree and I remember wondering how many seasons I might have to watch the leaves, budding, growing, changing colour and falling off. To this day that tree remains a very powerful mental image for me of the hopelessness you feel at times in prison.

The next morning, at breakfast time, a screw opened the hatch in the cell door and asked: 'What do you eat?'

In my naïvety I didn't realise that she was inquiring whether I was a vegetarian or not, so I said: 'I like roast chicken and pork, perhaps a little steamed or grilled fish.'

'Don't be funny,' she barked, 'I'm asking you are you vegetarian or ordinary diet?'

Well, this big blue plastic plate came through the hatch and on it was the smallest, skinniest, streakiest rasher of bacon I've ever seen in my life. It was about three inches long and shrivelled almost beyond recognition. There were two slices of dry bread on the plate and a knob of margarine.

'There's your breakfast,' said the screw. 'Do you want a cup of tea?'

I explained that I don't drink tea, so she told me that I could buy other drinks but, of course, I had no money.

I looked at that first meal and became convinced there and then that I would die of malnutrition long before I could complete my sentence.

When you first arrive in prison you are given one reception letter – a letter form for you to send free of charge to someone on the outside, just to let them know you are all right. My reception letter placed me in a dilemma. I had no money to buy stamps or paper. I had this one opportunity to communicate with the outside world, but to whom should it be?

After quite a bit of soul-searching I decided that my one and only precious letter would be sent to Ronnie.

While I was on remand and still visiting him regularly, I had told him that I had been nicked but it was nothing major to worry about. He respected my right to keep such matters to myself, so he didn't probe. By now, however, he must have read accounts of the trial in the newspapers, so I wrote to explain that I had not told him what serious trouble I was in because I didn't want to worry him, and I had always been convinced that at worst I would get no more than a two-year sentence.

The first three letters I got in Holloway all arrived in quick succession.

One was from Tony who chose to send me his reception letter to tell me that he was gutted and very worried about Sandra, but that he did not blame me in any way for what had happened. 'Keep your chin up,' he wrote. 'Keep your own counsel. Be careful who you mix with. These places are not nice and there are not many nice people inside, but you will find some. We will win our appeal and we'll be going home soon.'

Danny also wrote to say that he had heard the news and was distraught that I had been put away for such a long time. He also advised me to keep my own counsel and asked me to write to him.

The third letter, from Ron, was full of bile and bitterness against Brian: 'That bastard Thorogood,' he wrote, 'how could he do it to you? Why didn't you tell me you were in such bad trouble? I hope he comes here. I'll show him what I feel about what he's done to my girl.' Then he added a PS. 'I still love you. Don't worry.'

The first week in Holloway was a bit hazy, like a dream. They kept me locked up in my cell and just fed me through the hatch for the first few days because they were fearful of my reaction to the severity of my sentence. After all, I was now a convicted armed robber, an unknown quantity. Nobody knew if I was violent or likely to take my own life.

As soon as I was released from solitary all the girls rallied round. Our trial had been in all the papers with headlines like 'Black Widow and her gang get fifty years', so they'd read about me and were very sympathetic.

The fact that I was still wearing my silk court suit and plastic sandals was really depressing me. In those days there was no access to telephones for inmates, so one of the girls loaned me some paper and a stamp so that I could write to my family and get a set of clothes brought in. I sent a visiting order to my mum, telling her what I needed, and she brought in two towelling tracksuits, because they were the most practical, and a pair of slippers and a pair of trainers. On the next visit I swapped my silk suit, which had begun as an immaculate garment and now looked like something the cat had dragged in, for a shirt, a skirt and a pair of ordinary shoes for visits.

On my second week they took me to the canteen. Although I was allowed to spend up to £10 a month I had no money, so they explained that I would be given a 75p advance to offset against my prison wages when I began work. I thought 'Bloody hell, 75p. That won't go very far.'

Everyone who knows me knows that I am fanatical about my creams – hand creams, face creams, moisturising skin creams of all sorts. I was distraught that I was in prison without any. So I looked in the little Holloway canteen shop and I found a tiny tub of Astral cream for 48p and a bar of proper soap, and that was my first 75p gone.

A couple of days later I was interviewed by a panel of prison governors who baffled me with a barrage of dates and official jargon which boiled down to an estimation of the earliest and latest times I could expect to be released. I had been assessed, they said, and found suitable to be put on D3 Wing. At that time it was the best wing because it was where all those inmates who were allowed to work were housed.

When I arrived on the wing I was an object of curiosity because everyone had read about my case and they were all amazed at the length of my sentence. There were a couple of lifers in Holloway, but at that time the only other woman doing a seven stretch was Maggie Dunbar who was in for manslaughter.

The former prostitute began a torrid lesbian affair in the late 1970s with vice queen Christie Offord – known as Miss Whiplash. By agreement Maggie was artificially inseminated and had a son. Offord acted as the 'father and husband' in the relationship, but tried to have a sex change and began to behave more and more like a man. The pair split up after a bitter, violent row and Maggie set up a rival sex chamber and went back to work as a prostitute.

Shortly afterwards Offord's battered body was found in her sex parlour. She'd been throttled and bludgeoned with a metal bar. The bar was traced back to Maggie's flat, where it had last been seen, but it was two of Offord's clients who were charged with the murder and given life. Maggie was jailed for seven years for manslaughter and went to Holloway.

However, during this, her first period of detention in Holloway, Linda herself quickly made friends and began to adapt to prison life as she explains:

Everyone was really nice to me, lending me anything I needed and putting themselves out to show me the ropes. I was given a job as a wing cleaner, working with a girl called Steph Brown. I moved into a double cell with her and we became good friends.

Our resident governor on the wing at the time was a Mr Brown who was a very precise man and a stickler for rules. Most people found him intimidating but Steph, who had to clean his room, got on well with him. She told me that his desk was covered in objects which each had their precise place. She warned that if ever I had to clean the desk I should pick up each item individually, clean beneath it, and replace it in the same spot. Even then, she said, the pedantic Mr Brown would readjust the positioning.

When the day came that he called me in to clean, I forgot Steph's instructions until I had lifted all the objects from his desk and it was too late to memorise their positions. I thought I'd better start with the obvious so I gingerly replaced the blotter in the centre of the desk. Mr Brown stepped forward, moved it slightly and looked at me.

Then I began to imagine where, if it were my desk, I would place each object, but every time I put something down Mr Brown moved it to the other side.

The whole of this exercise was conducted in complete silence with nothing but eye contact between us after each move – a kind of bizarre slow dance around the desk.

When everything was back I said: 'Mr Brown, next time you ask me to clean your desk please remind me to take each item off one at a time, so that I can get it back in its right place.'

'But why Linda?' he asked. 'I'm not a fussy man.'

I just burst out laughing and it broke the ice between us. From then on we got on famously.

Everyone on the wing had a job except for one woman whose name was Maureen Kearney. She didn't work because she had refused to and everyone, staff and inmates alike, were terrified of her. For some reason, though, Maureen liked me and always chatted to me while I was working.

Linda's fellow wing cleaner, Steph Brown, was serving four years for her role as the female half of a Bonnie and Clyde couple who set up three shotgun raids while her male accomplice was on a weekend pass from a twelve-year jail sentence.

Her partner, former French Foreign Legion sergeant Matthew Porterfield got eight years in April 1986 after he had turned supergrass to help police solve a series of crimes in London and the Midlands. As a result the judge ordered that Porterfield's sentence should run concurrently with the twelve-year term so that he could be released in 1990. His common-law wife and her three children were rehoused after an underworld contract was put out on him.

Steph Brown met Porterfield when she was visiting another prisoner at Albany Jail on the Isle of Wight. Romance blossomed and when he was given his weekend pass he made straight for her home in Barnet, Hertfordshire. She introduced him to another man, Jeffrey Pollock, and they planned raids at a bank, a post office, and a pub which netted £16,000.

Pollock was jailed for ten years. Steph Brown, then aged forty-two, admitted taking part in the robbery at the post office and was alleged to have persuaded Porterfield not to return to prison to finish his sentence.

Linda takes up the story again:

Steph was the senior inmate on the wing at the time – known as a Blue Band because of the armband worn to denote her extra status.

When her sentence ended Mr Brown called me in and said: 'I've got good news and bad news. The good news is that you are promoted to Blue Band. The bad news is that this Blue Band is going to be a one-man band because I've got nobody left to share the cleaning work with you.'

When Maureen Kearney heard what he'd said to me, she stormed into his room and said: 'You cheeky bastard, telling her she's a one-man band. She isn't a one-man band anymore because I'm going to work with her.'

'But Maureen, you don't work,' he spluttered.

'Well, I do now,' she said and from then on she became The Wing Cleaner From Hell for all the staff. She wouldn't let them borrow milk or sugar for their tea, for instance.

I was in Holloway for a year and eventually I moved to A5 Wing which was the top of the shop. There was an officer up there who couldn't stand me. We nicknamed her Lipstick because she certainly slapped it on – thick and bright and very red.

Mr Brown had moved up to the wing with us, so when I knew my appeal was approaching I asked him if he would be the one to tell me the result because I didn't want to hear it from Lipstick.

He promised that he would handle it for me, but when the time came he was away on holiday. I kept asking Lipstick all day long if there was any news, but she denied all knowledge. At the very end of the day, when we were back in our dormitory, she just banged on the door and yelled through the hatch: 'Calvey, you've got two years off.'

'I said, "Thanks, what about my brother?" '

But she had already walked away.

The next day I asked her to change my record card to five years, so that everyone in the prison system would know that I was just doing five years instead of seven. That was important because so many things, like parole and movements between prisons, are calculated on length of sentence and depend on everyone knowing how long you are in for. But when Mr Brown came back from holiday he commiserated with me that my sentence had not been reduced. When he heard that it had, but my card had not been altered, he wanted to find out why it had not been done and made her work out all my new earliest release dates so that I could move on to a better prison.

During that first year in Holloway I met Ashley Fitts for the first time. She was only young and was doing two years for printing counterfeit car tax discs. The first time I saw her she was on the painting party. Everybody called her 'Bobble' because she wore a bobble hat to do her painting and looked like a little girl. I'd heard that she was very scared of being in prison, so I tried to chat to her as I was cleaning near to where she was painting. I offered to make her a drink, but she declined and later I heard that she'd been asking the other girls about me because she couldn't believe I was really an armed robber. I seemed too nice, she said.

In the first letter I had from Ron, after he had exploded over what he wanted to do to Brian, he told me to tell the Governor that I was his common-law wife and to apply for internal visits. I did as he instructed, but it was seven months before I was taken to Gartree top security prison to see my Ron.

I was as nervous as hell going to see him. As far as Ron was concerned, he'd trusted Brian to look after me. He was not bothered about us being together, but Brian wasn't flavour of the month. Ron still blamed him for getting me involved.

I was driven to Gartree Prison in Market Harborough, Leicestershire. I knew Ron was seething. I didn't know how he was going to react to me. When we arrived I was taken into the men's reception room. The visits at Gartree are held in the main hall with all the other visitors. However, as I was a prisoner too, I had to go into the male prisoners' waiting room. I was really embarrassed sitting with them, waiting to go in. All the prisoners were kind to me though, saying, 'Come on girl, you'll be all right.'

As I walked into the visiting hall all the other visitors were looking up, waiting anxiously for their husbands or boyfriends. When I came out of the prisoners' door wearing my blue towelling tracksuit they all stared and I thought, 'I bet they all think I'm a transvestite.'

Ron was waiting for me with a pile of newspaper clippings under one arm and a box of chocolates under the other. He never was a kiss and cuddly sort of a person, but when I walked up to him he bent and kissed me gently on the cheek. Then he growled a bit and said, 'How do you think I feel? Men do bird for armed robbery, not women.'

I told him I was sorry. I didn't mean to mug him off. But he wasn't angry with me. He had the raving hump with Brian for involving me. He sat all the way through the visit with the box of chocolates under his arm. Just as I was leaving, he said, 'By the way, these are for you. Do you still love me?'

I laughed and said, 'I never stopped loving you, you silly bastard.'

In all Linda served three years of her five year sentence and after she was granted parole she was transferred to East Sutton Park – a women's open prison in Kent, located south of Maidstone.

One of her most regular visitors at that time was Samuel Sapiano, a former armed robber and long-standing friend of her first husband Micky Calvey, having met him while serving a lengthy prison sentence. As an aside it is worth noting that Sapiano made legal history and set a precedent in 1978 when the Court of Appeal cut his fifteen-year jail sentence.

In making his judgement Lord Justice Lawton said he regarded Sapiano as a man who should be 'kept out of circulation for a very long time', but the court had no option other than to reduce the sentence to twelve years on the extraordinary grounds that another judge had led him to expect a reduction. In granting Sapiano and two other men leave to appeal four months earlier, Lord Justice Ormrod had indicated that their sentences should be 'substantially reduced'.

Sitting with Mr Justice Caulfield and Mr Justice Hodgson, Lord Justice Lawton said: 'Had it not been for what happened in July, the approach of this court would be entirely different.' The sentences recommended by Lord Justice Ormrod 'do not fit in with our views as to what would be appropriate, but these men have come here today expecting to get their sentences substantially reduced.' If they were disappointed it would 'give the appearance that something was wrong with the administration of justice from the mere accident that this court is differently constituted.'

In April 1973 Sapiano, then in his early thirties, had taken part in an £8,000 payroll robbery. In October that year he had stolen £6,000 from a mail van, and in June 1975 he had taken part in a security van raid.

Linda takes up the story:

Towards the end of my time at East Sutton Park I was being allowed weekend home leaves and my friend Sammy Sapiano invariably was the one to collect me. He used to pick me up in his gold Rolls-Royce which had a fitted mobile telephone – a rare luxury in the late nineteen-eighties – and drive me straight to Maidstone where Ronnie was in prison.

The routine was always the same. We went into the shops in Maidstone where Sammy would buy me some new clothes and we'd have a meal together before going in to visit Ron. Then Sammy would drive me up to London to spend the weekend with my family. On Monday Sammy would drive me down early so that I could get in to see Ron before I went back to prison.

East Sutton Park is housed in a beautiful Elizabethan manor house at the end of a majestic drive. The girls used to love watching for the visitors to arrive and would make all sorts of catcalls to me when they spotted Sammy's Rolls-Royce sweeping up the drive.

At the same time as me, there was a right posh lady in East Sutton Park. She was nice. I liked her. She was something high up in the horse racing world, but she was doing time for millions and millions of pounds worth of tax evasion. She had a navy-blue chauffeur-driven Rolls-Royce. When it came time for her home leaves, she would struggle to the door with all her bags, but as soon as she was outside her chauffeur would step forward and say: 'Madam, allow me.'

When her car and Sammy's car both arrived at the same time the screws' faces were a picture. You could imagine them thinking: 'We must be doing something wrong here.'

At the time of my release my sister Maxine, who lived around the corner from my house, went to an Ann Summers party in the neighbourhood. She overheard a discussion among several of the partygoers complaining that the tone of the area was being lowered because a woman who'd been in prison for armed robbery had moved into the next road.

Without declaring that she was my sister, Maxine took up the cudgels on my behalf and challenged how anyone could know that a neighbour had just come out of prison. It then emerged that a local resident was a Holloway prison officer and had been gossiping about me to her neighbours. That news made me a little paranoid and I began to imagine that everyone was looking at me and recognising me as a jailbird.

While I'd been in prison, my other sister Shelley had bought and renovated an old house in King George Avenue in Canning Town. She was preparing to sell it and move on, so I decided it was a perfect opportunity to make a fresh start where nobody knew who I was. I sold my house and bought Shelley's.

It was in a quiet little cul-de-sac with a school at the end. The garden backed on to hospital grounds and the front faced a park so the house was not overlooked. It is rare in the East End that you can look out on green on both sides and not have traffic roaring by all the time.

Shelley had made the house lovely, but I wanted to have a lot more done to it, so I went to see Ron. I told him that I'd found the ideal home for us both to live in when he came out. He was a keep-fit fanatic and the parks would have been perfect for his daily jogging.

Ron ordered a man, who was looking after his money while he was away, to pay for decorators to completely redo the house exactly as I wanted it. I had a huge patio made at the back and put marble on the walls. There were crystal chandeliers everywhere and the bathroom was decorated in a Victorian style. It was beautiful. I made it into my dream home. The dream turned into a nightmare, however, because that was the house where Ron died.

In fact the renovation of this house turned into a key factor in the Ronald Cook murder trial. The prosecution argued that over the years while he was in prison, Linda Calvey had been systematically spending Cook's ill-gotten gains without his knowledge. One of the motives for killing him, they suggested, was her fear of his reaction when he spotted the expensive house improvements and realised that his lover had effectively stolen all his wealth. This case was strengthened when Cook's alleged 'banker' gave evidence denying that Cook had ordered him to pay for Calvey's home renovations and pouring scorn on any suggestion that he had supplied a team of decorators to do the work.

By now Linda was re-establishing herself after her jail term. She recalls:

After Ashley came out of Holloway she set up her own printing business in north London but it went bust. So, once I had got back on my feet, I got a loan and lent it to her so she could start up a new business. We rented space in one of my brother's arches at Ironbridge Wharf near Canning Town flyover and she bought all the machines. I started working down there with her, but I knew nothing about printing so I decided to find something else to do.

While I was in East Sutton Park I had attended a soft furnishings course and discovered that I was a dab hand at making curtains. My sister Maxine is very artistic, so we decided to start a soft furnishings business together. Between us we had a few good contacts and we quickly established a good client base.

I got us a commission from a friend of mine who owned a wine bar in Romford. It was closed for renovation, so he gave us the job of supplying all the new curtains.

At the re-opening party, when it came to the speeches thanking all the contractors involved in the renovation, my friend finished by saying, 'And last but not least, a big thank you to Linda Calvey for the beautiful curtains.' At this some toerag at the back of the room piped up, 'Let's face it, if she'd hung sacks up in the windows we'd have had to have said they were beautiful.' Everyone roared with laughter.

Roy 'Pretty Boy' Shaw, the famous bare-knuckle fighter, was at the party and he came up and asked me to do his curtains. He took me and one of my ex-Holloway girlfriends, who was also at the party, straight back to his bungalow in Epping that night to measure up. He said, 'I can't believe two such lovely ladies as you could have been in prison. You both seem far too nice.'

In fact Linda could not have found a better customer than Roy Shaw if she wanted her curtain-making business to take off in the close-knit east London and Essex communities, where criminals and showbiz stars rub shoulders and vie for the greatest celebrity amongst their peers. Given the name Pretty Boy because of his film-star good looks when he was younger, and now a wealthy businessman, Shaw was once the most feared man in east London. During a jail term for armed robbery he was branded the most dangerous and violent inmate in the whole penal system. Even Broadmoor's infamous Dungeons – the punishment blocks at the hospital for the criminally insane – failed to break him.

He was so violent that even the Kray twins treated him with respect.

Outside prison, he was a ruthless street-fighting champion who struck fear into the hearts of all his opponents. He beat legendary underworld enforcer Lenny 'The Guv'nor' McLean, who described him as 'the hardest bastard I ever met'.

In his autobiography, which I wrote with him three years ago, Roy told how Great Train robber Ronnie Biggs offered him the chance to escape from Wandsworth jail with him for £10,000. He decided against the daring bid. 'Ten grand was just the price to go over the wall,' he said. 'Then there was the cost of a forged passport and money and tickets to go abroad. There were many times in prison when I envied Biggsy and wished I'd taken him up on his offer, but I could never have stayed away from Blighty for so long.'

As a client and advocate of Linda's business, Roy Shaw with his gentlemanly approach ('In my world you don't mistreat women and children. And you don't try and take liberties with me either') was clearly going to be an advantage.

Linda explains:

After I did Roy's curtains the business really picked up and we took on my aunt to help out. We got commissions for several pubs and shops and large houses and as each job finished another one started. It was all on word of mouth. I also had a hand in helping Ashley with her printing business.

I was really pleased with myself for the way I had got back on my feet after being in prison. I had a lovely little home and a nice little car and I thought at long last I was doing something straight that I enjoyed. Things were definitely looking up and I was looking forward to Ron coming home soon. He was constantly saying how proud he was of me for getting myself together after all I'd had to contend with.

One day when I went down to visit Ron in Maidstone he was pacing up and down *outside* the gates, waiting for me.

I was amazed to see him standing there on the pavement, so I pulled up and wound the window down. Ron had an urgent look on his face. 'Quick! quick! quick!' he whispered, 'let me jump in the motor. Now drive off. Go! go! go!'

I was in a panic. 'Why, what's happened?' I yelled.

'The screws made a mistake. They thought I was another prisoner due for release today and they've locked me *out*. I'm free. Let's go.'

'Oh no, Ron,' I said, 'we can't do this. You can't go on the run. Every Old Bill in the country will be looking for you within the hour.'

At that he just burst out laughing.

'I'm only winding you up,' he giggled. 'I've got a new job. I'm allowed out each day to clean at the pre-release hostel in the town.'

'What does that mean?' I asked.

'It means, Princess, you haven't got to come in and visit me anymore. I go in to the hostel first thing in the morning, do my cleaning, then, when all the people in the hostel go out to work, the rest of the day is my own until I go back to prison to sleep at night.'

So, we spent a lovely few hours wandering around Maidstone and from then on we used to take days shopping, having lunch and a few drinks. He even joined a health club and used the gym. As we became bolder we ventured further afield from Maidstone on his days out and eventually we took the bull by the horns and began going back to the East End to see his friends and some of his old haunts.

The first time we did that I showed him the house and he loved it. I had made all the curtains myself and carefully chosen the chandeliers and all the decorations. Everything was beautiful, but when I asked him what he thought, he could only talk about the big picture I had on the windowsill in the front room. It was a colour portrait of the two of us drinking champagne on the Las Vegas trip. 'I am so touched by seeing that there,' he said. 'You had no idea I was coming here today and you had no need to have my photo in your home. That has really made me happy.'

Ron was not a one for having his photograph taken. In the whole of the time we were together we only had three pictures done of the two of us – this one, one on holiday at a taverna in Corfu, and one at a party in Brixton held at the home of a screw who was a friend of Ron's. Little did I know when I had my picture taken in the screw's house that not much later I would end up in Holloway myself. From time to time Ron and I used to go down to the Holloway prison officers' mess for dinner with this screw and his wife, and I never gave the women on the other side of the wall a second thought.

Then suddenly I found myself one of them.

9

THE SMELL OF THE GREASEPAINT

Brian Thorogood, now a rugged 62-year-old, came out of prison after his last term in 1992. He now lives in Hackney and, ironically, works as a security guard. His conversation is littered with bad language.

His affection and deep admiration for Linda Calvey are undiminished by the passage of time and shine through his wistful reminiscences. He accepts, almost as normal, that Linda has transferred her affections and married the young thug he himself introduced her to. In his gravelly voice he says:

I just love her to death. If you love someone, then their happiness is all that matters. I've got no problem with her marrying Danny Reece. If her happiness lies with him then so be it. That's love. As much as I love her, I'm happy for her that she's happy.

* * *

He recalls an early incident, soon after he met Linda when he scarcely knew her and had not yet fallen for her charms.

There is only one reason for thieving. I thieve to improve the quality of life so, for every pound that I earned thieving, 60p was invested somewhere. That's how I got to own all my warehouses.

Linda, and her sister-in-law Maureen, were finding it difficult to make ends meet and they were always nagging me for money, so I agreed to let them rob my warehouse. I let them talk me into robbing myself.

The idea was that I would take them up to the warehouse at midnight with a Transit van and they would have one hour to stuff as much as they could get into the van and they could have that to sell. It was the height of the summer season and the warehouse was crammed with goods – everything from a pin to an elephant. None of it was mine, of course, it all belonged to customers and was being stored in transit before being shipped out. There were millions of pallets in the warehouse and I didn't think these women could do much damage.

It was dark when we got up there and the guard dog was no problem 'cos he knew me.

I thought finding the good stuff was going to be like looking for a needle in a haystack but the very first pallet they went to contained jeans and from then on they never put a foot wrong in an hour. Somehow they just knew exactly which pallets to go to.

When it was all over I said to Linda, 'Come here, you.' She looked at me with a sweet expression and asked 'What, Precious?' in an innocent sort of way which I later learned meant she was up to something.

'How did you know exactly which pallets to go to?' I asked.

'Easy,' she said, 'I went through all the paperwork in the office

...a, aged 1

Linda, aged 7

...da (right) aged 16, with her parents and the family

Linda, aged 22, in a typically provocative pose. What she likes to call her 'Hoochie Mamma' look

key Calvey looking every inch the gangster in the early seventies. This picture
s pride of place on Linda's cell wall. 'Everybody remarks on how like Burt
nolds he looks', she says

A rare photograph of Linda and Ron Cook together, taken on their romantic trip to Las Vegas in 1980

The Welford girls: Linda with mother and four sisters. From to right: Linda, Vivienne, Maxi Eileen (mother), Shelley and Ha

Linda and fellow 'lifer' Susan May, jailed for the murder of her aunt, mock their life behind bars in this pose snapped by a prison officer at Durham jail in the early nineties

Danny Reece in his cell at Wakefield prison showing off cuddly toys sent to him as love tokens by Linda

The bride and groom toast each other after their marriage in Durham's prison ch
1 December 1995

The happy couple with some of their guests.

Linda's son Neil and daughter Melanie protesting outside the Old Bailey after her conviction

A family picnic inside the grounds of HMP Durham in 1995. Left to right: Linda's son-in-law Martin, daughter Melanie, grand-daughter Sammy, Linda, son Neil and Neil's girlfriend Louise

Linda in her 'Not the Black Widow' outfit which won first prize for fancy dress at Durham's H-wing Christmas Party in 1993

'Ma' and other lifers at a p to celebrate the release of bombers Ella O'Dwyer Martina Ande

earlier in the day and noted down the pallet numbers that we wanted.'

That was Brian's first indication of the quality of the criminal brain which Linda possesses. They would soon team up as armed robbers and eventually she would become the senior partner – effectively the leader of the gang. Brian says:

We made a good team! I'm a good robber and I can plan a robbery, but at the end of the day sometimes I don't see what I should see. Lin is very, very clever. She is the sort of person who could have been whatever she wanted to be in life, she's that brainy.

Linda always said to me: 'Don't look to look. Look to see things. For example, run over and ask that bloke what the time is. I bet he can't tell you. He'll have to look at his watch. He'll not look to look he'll look to see.'

When I was doing armed robberies I would go and look at the target five or six times, but when Linda was with me she would be taking note of things I missed. She would say to me: 'You're making so many mistakes, you silly boy. You're losing money.'

With armed robberies you can't be responsible for your partner. If you are you might lose half a million. I was working with a team of nice people, but they weren't very good and I was losing money hand over fist. I once trusted a bloke to watch the delivery of cash to a post office. He said only one cash box went in. When we robbed it, I stood with my back to the van and he told me when the box had gone in. What he had not noticed was that there was always a delay and the guards came out and took two more boxes in. Anyway, by robbing just one box when I could have had three I lost £50,000.

Now Linda will know what's best for you but she won't tell you. She'll wait 'til you see it for yourself. I didn't realise that she had been a thief for years because I wasn't looking. One day we were in a supermarket at dinnertime when the staff were on a break and the safe was full. She told me to wait by the door, which I did, but I happened to be at an angle where I could see into the office and I saw her calmly walk in, rob the office, put the keys back, put the money in her bag, walk out, and finish her shopping.

I started out using her as a getaway driver, but she was so reliable she began to take a bigger part. People say you couldn't trust a woman on a robbery. It was never dangerous to have Linda on a robbery with me. I always felt safe as houses with her.

Out of loyalty Brian will not detail Linda's armed robbery exploits, but it is clear that she was one of the main gun-wielding robbers herself.

She carried a gun and, let me tell you, it was not for show. She was not afraid to use it. With most of the men on my team the gun was for show only. They weren't going to shoot anyone, so why bother?

Basically, at the end she was the number one on the team and I was the number two. She was the boss. We worked for her. She planned it all and ran it all. We were putting our liberty in her hands. If she got one thing wrong or she didn't do the job properly we would get nicked.

She had this brilliant idea that the police would not expect us to strike twice in the same place, so for a while we were doing double robberies – robbing the place one day then going back to the same place the day after. We didn't need guns the second day. The staff would know what to expect and just line up, put their hands on their heads, hand over the keys, and let us take what we wanted.

What I did was the groundwork in the areas to identify the post offices that looked a good bet to rob and then I left the rest to Linda. I would pick out about five bits of work – targets like post offices or security vans – then reject two and pick the main target from the remaining three, with the other two in reserve.

Once I'd done that, I would go round to one or two people I

trusted and offer them a bit of work, without telling them who else was on the team or what the target was.

My only worry was, what sort of a person was I, if we got nicked, to get a woman involved? So I said: 'Listen, because I love you it's got to stop.'

After that we got Carl, who was the driver who got nicked with us. He was recommended by a third party as someone who wanted a bit of work. I told Linda to go and find us a bit of work and then Carl and I would do it.

Just twice in their long affair did Brian see the vicious side of Linda – and both times it was in defence of him. He says:

We were in this pub once and she punched a guy who had said something about me she didn't like.

On another occasion she went missing for a couple of days, and when I got on her trail I was told that she was trying to track down a man who had been bad mouthing me. She had a gun and was determined to kill him. Everywhere I went she had been before me, but the geezer was on a bender himself and kept one step ahead of her. Eventually, I caught her just before she caught up with the guy.

She's just such a genuine person. She's warm and compassionate, but if she says she loves you then anyone who harms you or behaves like your enemy is her enemy too and they are in trouble.

These days the epidemic of armed robberies which gripped London for more than two decades from the mid-seventies onwards has largely abated. Ten years ago the kind of people who committed armed robberies were not, in the main, opportunist criminals although they did represent a wide spectrum of types. Some were amateurs, mature in years, who had been forced into armed crime by financial pressures. Most of them, however, were people approaching the pinnacle of criminal achievement; they were professionals who had done a lot and were prepared to do more – dangerous people willing to carry a gun and use it without compunction.

Professional armed robbers have two main ways of robbing security vans. One is to threaten the guards when they are making deliveries and steal the bags of cash. The other is to hijack the whole van. In this method a gun is pointed at the head of a guard who is outside. The driver is then ordered to open up the van or his colleague will be shot. The security personnel will then be thrown out on to the pavement, or they will be locked in the back of the van while it is driven away. It will be taken to a place where the money can be taken from it – in the language of the trade the van will be 'slaughtered'.

Linda is understandably reluctant to talk in too much detail about her career as an armed robber, for fear that she might yet be charged with offences committed almost twenty years ago. However, she did tell me the remarkable story of how she took up the profession and, in general terms, how she went about her nefarious business. Her eyes shone and her voice took on a kind of schoolgirl excitement as she recounted her most daring escapades. I found her account oddly disturbing because it was devoid of remorse or any sense of guilt – quite the contrary, there was almost a sense of triumph. It was clear to me that Linda was the brains behind her robbery gang. She regarded the men who worked for her as ignorant dolts. They worshipped her with blind devotion, and when it came to the crunch even took the rap for her. They were clearly in awe of her and she ruled them with a ruthlessness which belied her sexy exterior.

Linda takes up the story:

I've never confided this to anyone before, but it was my Micky's death that turned me into an armed robber . . . not Ronnie Cook or Brian Thorogood.

Micky died trying to make a living for his children. He didn't want to go on that last job, I didn't want him to go, but it was coming up to Christmas and he had to go to make ends meet for the family.

When I saw him lying there in his coffin I bent down and kissed him gently on the forehead. I whispered that I loved him and then I made a vow to him. I was a young widow with two tiny children. I promised him that I would provide for his children and if that meant taking up his profession of armed robbery I would do it, even if I had to die the same way that he had done.

It was almost a year to the day after Micky's death that I carried out my first robbery.

I am a very methodical person, almost pedantic about detail, so it was very important to me to plan every robbery meticulously. I was not prepared to leave anything to chance.

Most robbers plan their operations with success in mind. All they allow for is the certainty that they will get away afterwards. I planned all my operations in the belief that I would get caught. With that approach in mind, I always carefully plotted a minimum of three escape routes.

It is a question of starting at the venue of the robbery, let's say in a street outside a bank, building society or post office, and working your way outwards from there. When the armoured cash van has arrived on the 'plot' the robbers will either be driven to the scene in the getaway car or they will be waiting in the street or nearby shops, dressed as casual shoppers, and only spring into action when the time is right. The getaway car will be driven to the outside of the bank, ready to take the robbers and the cash away. The gang will then drive to a nearby street where a second getaway car will be parked so that a switch can be made to foil any pursuers or any witnesses who might have noted the details of the original getaway car.

All of this, of course, requires split-second timing and a good system of signals between the various members of the gang. It takes weeks of watching, waiting and rehearsal to get it right.

I always planned on the assumption that the police had been tipped off and were lying in wait for us. If that were the case, they would have to allow us to complete the robbery before they moved or they would not have any evidence that we had done anything wrong. The point at which they would make their move would be when we attempted to get away in the getaway car. You had to assume that they would ambush us outside the bank by using vehicles to box us in and block the escape route. If that happened, we would need an escape route on foot. I would spend a considerable amount of time walking the shortest routes and those least likely to be blocked – alleyways, school playgrounds, car parks, churches, even shops which had back doors leading on to escape routes. I would walk through shops to the back and pretend to be lost or looking for a toilet if anyone challenged me. I was always looking for gates or doors which were routinely left unlocked but which could be locked behind us to stymie the police if they were in hot pursuit.

Having worked out the quickest and safest escape route on foot, I would then work out where to park the second, third and even fourth getaway cars. My assumption was that if the police knew about the raid, they would have been watching us in the days and hours leading up to it and so might have watched us park the getaway cars. That being the case, they would probably not only be waiting by the first switchover car, but they would also be watching the car I had placed at the end of the escape route on foot. So I always had a third car, parked strategically during the night several days before the raid, as a final fall-back position for us.

Simply choosing a parking for your getaway cars is a science in itself. First of all you must find a spot where a parked car will not contravene any traffic regulations. The last thing you want to find, when you need the car in a hurry, is that your escape vehicle has been either towed away or had its wheels clamped while you are carrying out the robbery. You must also find a place which will not annoy local residents or draw attention to the vehicle in any way – you don't want a nosey neighbour noting down the index number and complaining to the police. Then you must also ensure that there is enough space around the car so that other cars cannot inadvertently box it in.

Finally, and most importantly, you must ensure that there will be nothing blocking the road when you need to drive away fast. In that connection, I always took a careful note of the times when large vehicles like the dust cart, or lorries making regular deliveries, or even buses would be in that street so that we could avoid them. Ideally, I would also want a street with lots of streets leading off it, so that it would take more than two police cars to block our getaway route.

When it came to selecting the switchover point, I always looked for a short route on foot between the two cars which would prevent anyone driving after us – a pedestrian alley with bollards for instance. The favourites were building sites with a hole in the fence (sometimes I had to cut the hole myself during the night) or parks with a gap in the hedge.

After that, it was just a matter of getting the members of the team with the right skills to steal the cars, make sure they were full of petrol and the engines worked, and park them in the right places at the right time.

All that planning, of course, took place after I had selected the robbery target and worked out its feasibility. That part of the operation, naturally, took several months because I had to watch the arrival of the vans and time them very carefully. The vans would usually come at roughly the same time on particular days of the week, but their routines were subject to variation. I needed to know what time of day they arrived, and which immediate route they took to arrive at and to leave the location. I needed to know how many guards each van carried and exactly what their routine for delivering or taking away the cash was. I needed to know the points at which they were most vulnerable to attack and precisely how long their operation took from start to finish, in particular how long the money would actually be exposed to direct seizure. I also needed to know who could raise the alarm and how.

I did all of this research on my own, posing as a shopper, with a stopwatch in my pocket. I never trusted anyone else to do my planning for me. The reason it took so long was that I couldn't risk being seen at the same location every time the cash van was there. I had to have quite a few targets on the go at once, so that I could move around between them and make my researches without arousing suspicion.

Once all the planning was complete, I would then recruit my team, but only a matter of days, sometimes hours, beforehand so as to avoid any breaches of security. Each man knew only what he needed to know. I selected them on the basis of their personal skills – drivers, lookouts, armourers – and always the minimum numbers, usually no more than five or six people at the very most.

Once I'd got my team chosen I would bake a cake with some home-made biscuits and make a huge plate of sandwiches before inviting them all round to my house for tea. Then, while they sat in my living room scoffing their food, I would outline the plan to them. That usually involved spreading out maps on the carpet and actually role playing and timing moves with the stopwatch. I would make them dash into the kitchen or the hall while I yelled instructions at them.

Sometimes I felt a bit like a schoolmistress with a class of foolish schoolboys because I made everyone go over and over the plan until I was sure they had remembered every little detail and there was no room for mistakes.

When it came time to leave for the robberies, my routine was always the same. I always kissed each man and sent them off with the words 'Good luck boys!' I suppose it was a bit like a mother sending off a bunch of naughty little lads to take part in a school football match.

I think the men were intimidated by me and fearful of my wrath if they failed. I didn't always go on the robberies myself and once, I recall, I waited anxiously at home for my team who did not return at the time they should have. It was a complicated job I'd been planning for many months. Eventually, more than four hours late, they arrived.

I exploded, 'Where the hell have you lot been?'

'We couldn't do the job, it was too dangerous,' said one of the men. 'We knew you would be angry, so we thought we'd better do another one. We went to Ilford and did one of the back-up jobs we've been planning for a while.'

I just snorted, 'Get out the back, cut the top off the bag, and let's see what you've got.'

Years later, after my arrest, I learned that towards the end of my career as an armed robber the police rented a house two doors away from mine, on the other side of the street, so that they could keep me under surveillance. One detective told me how they would roar with laughter to see, for instance, a car pull up and three hefty muscle-bound men with broken noses get out and go into my house, only to re-emerge minutes later to clean the windows or shake out the rugs.

The fact was that when we were not engaged in an armed robbery I made full use of my gang members to help with my domestic chores. After all, I was a woman living on her own and, in order to command respect from the men around me, I had to be very strict with them about their behaviour. If they couldn't obey me when I wanted something done around the house, then they wouldn't obey in the heat of a robbery and that could prove disastrous.

In a strange way a robbery is very much like a theatrical production. It is certainly dramatic and requires a great deal of attention to detail to make it convincing. When you are engaged in it there is a surreal quality, you feel as though you are performing an act outside yourself or your normal everyday life which, of course, you are.

In order to make my operations as effective as possible, I had to have the appropriate props which I arranged to have stolen for me. I acquired so many over the years that eventually I had to have my own props store – a lock-up garage over in Bow. There I kept things like workmen's shelters – the red-and-white striped portable tents that electricians put up over manhole covers in the street. They were invaluable because we could put them up outside a bank and have our lookouts or even our gunmen sitting inside them, dressed in workmen's overalls and drawing no attention to themselves whatsoever.

To back all that up I had a whole range of council workmen's equipment – street sweepers' brooms, donkey jackets and boots, and road-closed or diversion signs which often helped us to keep unwanted traffic out of the way while we were carrying out a raid.

I also had a temporary bus-stop sign which was sometimes useful in two ways. If I wanted to keep buses out of the way and there was a bus-stop directly outside the bank, for instance, we would put an 'Out of Service' bag over the real sign and move the temporary one up the road out of the way, so that bus drivers would not stop and passengers would queue up further away from our intended target.

The other way I used the temporary bus-stop was to put it outside the target location so that I could pretend to queue up for a bus when I was actually watching the movements in the bank. One of my men, dressed in London Transport overalls, would drive up in a van and put the bus-stop down. He'd pick it up later and no one would be any the wiser.

The really fun part of all this for me, as a woman, was the use of disguises. In my prop store I had a whole range of wigs, hair dyes, and moustaches. The police and the prison authorities also keep careful records of criminals' distinctive marks, like tattoos and scars. I was able to have lots of fun by using theatrical make-up and temporary tattoos to give my team temporary physical identities – like scars on their faces and tattoos on their hands and arms – which witnesses would remember and report to the police.

The theatrical part was certainly the most enjoyable. Perhaps I am a frustrated actress. Once I managed to get hold of one of the artificial 'bumps' they use in the theatre to make women look pregnant. It was perfect for hiding a gun inside and I used it successfully to rob a Securicor van on my own by simply hanging around looking like an expectant mum until the guard came across the pavement carrying the bag. You should have seen the look on his face when I produced a gun from my tummy and ordered him to hand over the cash. He was so shocked I reckon he'd have given me the keys to the van itself without me having to ask.

On one occasion I had placed the temporary bus-stop sign outside a bank we were going to rob. I was inside the bank, very slowly filling in a paying-in slip while I waited for the security guards to arrive. The key member of our team was standing at the bus-stop with his balaclava and a sawn-off shotgun in his hold-all, ready to move in on the security guards when I gave the signal that they were leaving the bank on the way back to the security van.

As he stood there, two little old ladies with their shopping bags joined him. They were moaning about the weather and the long queue in the post office and they soon started chatting to the man at the bus-stop.

'I never knew there was a bus-stop here,' said one. 'Has it been here long?'

My man grunted a non-committal reply.

'This is really good, we won't have to walk so far with our shopping,' said the other old dear. Then came a torrent of questions: 'What bus stops here? How far are you going? Where do you live? Where have you come from? What are you doing?'

I couldn't hear the conversation, but from inside the bank I could see that my man was being distracted and the old ladies would be potential witnesses who could identify him afterwards. More importantly, if there was a shoot-out with the police, I didn't want old ladies in the line of fire. I decided to abort the robbery.

Walking out of the bank, I strolled up to my man. 'Hello Bill,' I said. 'Never mind waiting for the bus, Darling, I've got the car round the corner, I'll give you a lift. Where d'you want to go?'

As we walked away I heard one old lady say to the other, 'Lucky bugger. I wouldn't mind a lift meself. My feet are killing me.' Seconds later the security van rolled round the corner and pulled up outside the bank.

Looking back, it was an hilarious episode, but it could have been a disaster. We robbed that bank two months later.

There were many very funny moments in my robbery career.

As I built a reputation as a success I was being approached by men wanting to join my team. One such was a very skinny black man, well over six-foot tall. He looked like a Harlem Globetrotter basketball player. He was very short of money and begged me to let him take part in a robbery. He would do anything, he said.

Well, there was no way I could risk him being seen. He stood out like a sore thumb. I felt sorry for him, however, because he had little children to feed, so I relented and allowed him to accompany me on a robbery I had planned in Hornchurch. If he was there, he could claim a share of the takings, and in the future I might have been able to find him some useful work like stealing cars or something.

On that occasion I was the getaway driver. My black friend lay curled up on the back seat under a blanket. One of the gang members ran out of the bank, threw the bag of money into the back on top of him, then jumped into the front passenger seat, took off his balaclava and picked up a newspaper to read. The other gang members had another car to get away in. Once we were out of sight of the bank my friend in the back could sit up so that it looked like a husband and wife – the wife driving and the husband reading the paper – with a black friend being given a lift in the back.

Whenever I was driving away from a robbery I always kept the window down so that I could hear the sound of police car sirens approaching. It was always my policy to drive directly towards the police, never away from them, so as to avoid suspicion and prevent them assuming that I was making my escape and therefore had to be pursued. This particular day I heard them before I saw them, but when I spotted the two cars, headlights flashing, blue lights going, racing towards us, I deliberately took up a position which would obstruct their progress. Then, when the cars got up to us, like an incompetent woman driver, I made a show of pulling over and waving them through. Both police car drivers waved in acknowledgement of their thanks as they roared past. There was no way those officers would ever have suspected that we were the armed robbers making our getaway.

I looked in my rearview mirror to see my black friend's panic-stricken face.

'Have I gone white?' he stammered. 'Are you completely mad?'

I just hooted with laughter.

Sharing out the money was always done at my house over a drink. The routine was always the same. The tops would be cut off the money bags, or the lids of the cash boxes would be prised open, and the money tipped out on to the floor.

After I had counted it, I would take expenses to cover my overheads like cars, petrol, ammunition, weapons, props and so on. The remainder would then be divided equally between the members of the gang and they would each then give me back ten per cent of their cut from the pile of cash lying in front of them on the floor. As they left the house they would each get a kiss and a 'Well done, boys' from me and invariably they would slip me a wad of notes as an extra thank you.

Brian Thorogood, bless him, never took his share. He always handed the lot over to me, saying that he had only done the robbery for me. 'Give me £100 and I'll take you out for a meal afterwards,' was always his response when I urged him to take more.

My success as a robber was born of a total determination to seize back what was rightfully mine. I convinced myself that the money I was stealing had originally been stolen from me and other poor people like me – a kind of Robin Hood philosophy. I believed that I was not taking money from banks and other financial institutions to which I had no right. It was a kind of self-brainwashing and I was comfortable with the idea. The police had killed my husband and society owed me the right to make a good living by redressing the financial imbalance.

In the early stages of my relationship with Brian he used to take me on robberies as his getaway driver. On one occasion we went to rob a post office. Brian went in with the shotgun to do the job and I sat outside in the car with a ridiculous wig on as a disguise. Ten minutes went by, no Brian. Fifteen minutes went by, no Brian. Twenty minutes went by, no Brian. I was thinking: 'Where is he? What's happening?' I could see people going into the post office and I thought: 'It must have all come on top,' but I was determined not to leave. Since then I've acquired a reputation for having nerves of steel, but first and foremost I wouldn't leave a friend in the lurch so I wasn't going to let Brian down.

What had happened was that there was a time-delay lock fitted to the post office safe which meant a half-hour wait from the time its code was deactivated by the postmaster until the safe door could actually be opened. Throughout that time Brian was crouching out of sight beneath the counter, with a gun pressed into the groin of the postmaster who was obliged to carry on serving customers as if nothing was happening.

Brian kept his nerve and so did I, and we got away with the

money, but it taught me a valuable lesson about the importance of thorough research before carrying out any crime.

It is amazing how little old ladies seem to be the ones that invariably and inadvertently find themselves at the centre of armed robberies. Once I did a job with Brian and two other men at a post office in Essex. We waited until the cash box had been delivered and then the other two raced in with shotguns to conduct the robbery while Brian and I waited outside in the car. Just then a tiny little old lady, looking about ninety, tottered towards the front door.

'Please don't go in, please walk on,' whispered Brian. But in she went. 'Oh God, what can we do now?' he said.

I just screamed at him. 'Get in there and take her hostage. Do it now!'

Inside, he grabbed the old dear, put a gun to her head and yelled: 'Hand over the money now or I'll kill her.' Then he bent down and whispered in her ear: 'Don't worry, Darling, I'm not going to hurt you, whatever happens.'

She was a feisty old thing who was clearly enjoying the drama and determined to make the most of it by playing the part of a hostage to the full.

'Give them the money,' she shouted to the post office staff. 'They must be desperate. Don't give them the little notes, give them the big notes.'

Afterwards we tried to track her down because the lads wanted to give her £2,000 as an appreciation.

Once I got into the swing of armed robberies I couldn't wait for the adrenaline rush it gave me. I loved the buzz of picking up a shotgun and confronting men in armoured vans and protective clothing and forcing them to hand over vast sums of money. It was like a drug and I got more and more daring as time went on. I very rarely failed and if I did I always went back and did the same target later.

10

A MARRIAGE MADE IN CELLS

Danny Reece is one of the most dangerous men in the prison system. He is a big, powerful man with a vile temper. He is a loner who cares for nobody and doesn't care what anyone thinks of him. Cross him and you may not live to regret it.

Where Linda Calvey gets her own way behind bars by deploying the full range of her feminine wiles, Danny, a body-builder and fitness fanatic, simply batters the system into submission through his physical presence and reputation for making trouble. He once ripped a cell door off its hinges and no inmate will dare box against him because he is too strong ever to be felled, even by the most powerful blows.

Together they make a formidable couple. No one messes with 'Ma' Calvey, but if they should have the temerity to take her on they would have to reckon with her muscular husband too.

Danny's criminal career started with petty thieving but soon escalated. By the early 1980s he was married with three young sons. Still in his mid-twenties, he already had a record for armed robbery when he discovered that his wife was having an affair with a neighbour. Enraged by this, Danny stormed the family home of his wife's lover and held everyone inside hostage at gunpoint. During the course of several days of physical and mental torture he strung people up on the banisters.

In 1986 he was given a 13-year sentence for false imprisonment.

Three years later, he gained public notoriety for the first time during the high-profile Janie Shepherd murder trial.

Janie was the beautiful blonde Australian heiress, step-daughter of a prominent Sydney banker, who was abducted in her Mini from outside her home in London's fashionable Maida Vale in February 1977. After a lengthy hue and cry her body was discovered ten weeks later on Normansland Common, a popular Hertfordshire beauty spot.

She had vanished after setting out to visit her boyfriend, cricketer Rodney Kinkead Weekes, at his Knightsbridge home. How she had been killed and the identity of her killer was to remain a mystery for eleven years, until Danny Reece, by then held in Frankland Jail in Durham, asked for a private interview with the police.

Reece told astonished detectives that another inmate, sex offender and fellow body-builder David Lashley, then serving an 18-year sentence for rape, had confessed to him that he was Janie's killer. The pair had become friendly during weightlifting sessions in the prison gym.

Lashley, he said, had grown angry while reading press reports of a man being sentenced to life for rape and said that the man should have killed his victim in the same way that he had killed Janie after abducting her and raping her at knife-point.

During a lengthy trial at St Albans Crown Court doubts were raised over Reece's reliability as a witness and his motivation for becoming a police informant, but it emerged that Lashley, a former van driver, had made a similar confession to Robert Hodgson in Wakefield Prison in 1981. Hodgson only came forward after learning of Reece's statement to the police. In the event, Lashley was convicted of Janie's murder and jailed for life.

After their convictions Reece and Linda kept in close touch through inter-prison visits. Every three months Danny was allowed to travel from the top-security Whitemoor Prison in Cambridgeshire to Durham where he would stay in male quarters.

The first indication the world had that Linda intended to marry her co-murderer came in a short newspaper story just three years after the couple were found guilty of Ronnie Cook's killing. In January 1994 under the headline 'Murder Widow Calls off Wedding', the *Sunday People* reported:

> Black Widow Linda Calvey has called off her bizarre prison wedding to the man who helped murder her common-law husband. The 45-year-old killer was given special permission to marry behind bars on Valentine's Day.
>
> But now she and Daniel Reece, 37, who are both serving life, have suddenly cancelled the ceremony. It is understood they now plan to wait until their release before marrying.
>
> Friends refused to comment on the reason for the change of heart. But a Home Office spokesman said: 'They were concerned about their children.'
>
> The couple had planned to wed at Parkhurst Prison on the Isle of Wight where Reece is serving his sentence.
>
> A Parkhurst source said last night: 'It must have been the devil who played Cupid. It is a marriage straight from Hell.'

By the time the news reached the outside world, however, Linda had been plotting to get her man for quite some time. She recalls:

I first proposed to Danny when he was in Parkhurst and I was up in Durham. He refused me and I was quite taken aback, but I was determined not to give up, so I left it a little while and asked him again. Again he said 'No.' It wasn't until the third time of asking that he finally agreed. We set about making plans for the wedding to take place in the prison chapel at Parkhurst.

Everything was organised down to the last detail: the wedding cake was made, the banns had been read, he'd asked one of his friends to be best man and Kate loaned me her wedding outfit that she'd worn when she married Ron Kray. At the last minute Danny changed his mind. He couldn't go through with it, so the wedding was called off.

At the time we had a really nice Governor in charge of the lifers at Durham called John Smith. His hobby was photography and he offered to take pictures of me in Kate's wedding outfit as a little keepsake. So I had a full set of photos done of me all by myself – my 'I never got married' pictures. Perhaps it was just as well that we didn't get married that time because I later heard that a public protest was planned on the Isle of Wight against allowing people like us to get married in a church. You'd think people would worry about themselves wouldn't you, not what other people are doing. Fancy begrudging people who are locked up the opportunity to get married in a church. I was a widow and Danny was a single man, so we were entitled to get married in a church.

Actually Linda already had two high-profile suitors behind bars who were vying with Reece for her hand in marriage.

Twice a week she exchanged telephone calls with Reg Kray. He would call Durham Prison from Maidstone Jail leaving a message for Linda to 'call me at my office'. She would often respond by leaving messages for him saying: 'You can ring me back at my office.'

These telephone calls became increasingly intimate and eventually

Reggie proposed to Linda – a proposal he repeated several times until it became clear that she intended to marry Reece instead.

Her other admirer was the notorious prison hardman Charlie Bronson. Bronson is considered Britain's most dangerous convict. During almost thirty years inside, he has gained a fearsome reputation as the prison service's only serial hostage-taker. He has spent twenty-two years in solitary confinement, yet has never killed anybody. His original crime was armed robbery, but his disruptive behaviour in prison has seen more and more years added to his sentence. He jokes: 'I've been on more roofs than Santa Claus, eaten more porridge than Goldilocks and the Three Bears, and taken more hostages than Saddam Hussein.'

He does 3,000 press-ups a day and is the six-time winner of the Koestler Award for prison art for his brilliant, innovative and disturbing cartoons. A prolific letter writer, Bronson was attracted to the image and personality of Linda Calvey as portrayed in the press and began a regular correspondence with her.

Soon he proposed marriage and repeated the proposal on a monthly basis. When told that she intended to marry Danny Reece, Bronson wrote back: 'You can have two husbands. You can have him for sex and I'll just live in a shed at the bottom of the garden for company.'

It was a theme he returned to after her marriage, although he has since wed a young Asian woman, becoming a Muslim and changing his name to Ali in the process.

Despite this flattering attention, Linda was determined to marry Reece and refused to let his sudden attack of cold feet stand in the way. She recalls:

When I next saw Danny on a visit I gently asked him why he'd called the marriage off. He simply said, 'It's not because I don't love you, I love you more than anything on this earth. I just don't feel worthy of you.' I was touched by his devotion but told him not to be so silly. I said, 'Look, this is the fourth and last time I am going to ask you, will you marry me?' When he said 'Yes', I said, 'Right you'd better come up and marry me in Durham then this time.' He laughed and said, 'Yeah, I think I'd better. Then I can't get away can I?'

So once again we set about organising.

When it came to it the 1995 wedding raised a storm of protest and attracted very hostile press coverage with headlines like 'Shotgun Wedding' and 'This bride's a killer, her groom is a murderer, and one of the bridesmaids is a torturer'. The newspapers reported that the bridesmaids wore black as a sign of respect for the wicked bride who herself chose a virginal white dress in stark contrast to her dark Black Widow outfits. One inmate told the *News of the World*: 'Her dress must have cost a fortune. She looked stunning.'

On the morning of the ceremony I had flu and couldn't attend. According to the *News of the World* the wedding, conducted by prison chaplain Rev. Michael Dixon, was

> the social highlight for inmates of Durham's H Block.
>
> She walked up the aisle to the sound of the Righteous Brothers' hit 'Unchained Melody'. The best man was prison governor Mike Martin and the wedding photographer was a retired warder.
>
> John Smith who took the pictures recalled: 'Linda wrote and asked if I'd do it. I advised against but they seemed determined to get married.'
>
> After the service the wedding party adjourned to a visiting room decorated with pink ribbon and flowers, where guests tucked into a buffet.
>
> Inmates had made sausage rolls, pies, salads, chocolate gateaux and a tiered wedding cake.

The couple were allowed to kiss and cuddle and cheering cons threw confetti. Afterwards Reece was shipped back to his jail.

A prison insider said: 'It was incredible to think all this was going on in a prison. It is the lunatics running the asylum.

'There's thousands of young couples who wouldn't have had as good a wedding as they did. It's disgusting really. It's not as if they are going to be setting up home together. Why go to all the expense for a couple of murderers? It's not right that she was allowed to marry him in the chapel because of who she is and what she did.

'Many people in the Prison Service are sick of killers getting what they want. It's scandalous. Their feelings shouldn't be respected – they had no sympathy for their victims.'

Another insider revealed: 'Everybody was looking their best. It was all very traditional. All the congregation – the inmates – were looking nice and smart as well. It was a very sensitive occasion, a really good service.'

A prison officer explained: 'Up here we treat them all as just another prisoner. High-risk inmates are our bread and butter. The Prison Service doesn't stop them marrying if they want to. It's up to them. The only reason it was at the church was to save us all the risk of two Category A prisoners marrying at the nearby register office.'

No doubt all of this brought a smile to the face of publicity-needy Linda. She takes up the story of her special day as she remembers it:

Durham is a very austere prison, one of the most claustrophobic atmospheres you could imagine to live in. It was condemned for men years ago, but still women prisoners live there for many years on end.

The Number One governor at Durham then was a Mr Mitchell who was very sympathetic to the women. I gave my list of the things I wanted to Governor Smith and he and Mr Mitchell agreed to virtually everything. The only thing that was turned down was my request for the ceremony to be video-recorded on the grounds that so many high-profile inmates would be attending. I had asked permission to invite every girl in the women's H Wing and they agreed. It was easier for the authorities that way than if I'd just invited my friends, which would have set up resentments throughout the whole block. I reckon my wedding guest list must be unique because it included Rose West and Myra Hindley – two of the most notorious female killers in history. In the event neither of them made it to the wedding because they were both confined to the hospital wing. Myra had broken her leg in two places as a result of the osteoporosis she's suffered from in recent years and Rose was being treated for chronic depression over her situation. Myra sent a lovely little note wishing me well and saying how much she would have loved to have been there. It would certainly have been interesting to have had those two featuring in my wedding photographs. When I later saw Rose, I gave her the Floral decoration from the top of the cake as a memento.

Preparations for the wedding caused great excitement among the girls and everybody set about either making themselves new outfits or sending off for new clothes from home. It was the biggest event in all our lives.

I paid for everything. I'd been saving up for ages and not a penny of public money was spent on my wedding. I was allowed to choose the food I wanted, because at the time the staff used to go out and shop for us. I was only allowed a wedding cake made by an authorised person – to stop anyone smuggling something like drugs or weapons in I suppose – so I ordered mine from Mrs Hellens, a lady who worked in the prison and made cakes professionally. We decided on a two-tier cake.

The Governor agreed to my request for four bridesmaids, but by the time the wedding took place two of the girls had been shipped out to other prisons, so I ended up with two killers – Bernie McNeilly, who was one of the 'Chucky' murderers, and Maria Smith, who had been dubbed by the press 'The Devil's Daughter'. As a young girl growing up and dreaming of one day being married I certainly didn't envisage having bridesmaids like that! Then again, I never imagined being called The Black Widow myself. Incidentally, Bernie McNeilly is one of the loveliest girls I've ever met. She is so nice and not a bit the way the press have portrayed her.

In fact Bernadette McNeilly was jailed for life in 1993 after leading a sadistic gang that killed sixteen-year-old Suzanne Capper in a vicious act of revenge. Suzanne's 'crime' had been to lose a coat belonging to McNeilly.

Bernadette, at the time a 23-year-old mother of three, chillingly acted out scenes from the horror movie *Child's Play III* featuring an evil doll come to life called Chucky.

At McNeilly's trial in Manchester the jury heard that the victim Suzanne had been stripped naked, beaten, shackled to a bedframe, tortured with cigarette ends, injected with drugs and had bad teeth pulled out with pliers.

McNeilly mocked her victim by chanting: 'Chucky's gonna play,' like the doll in the film.

Finally the agonised girl was dumped in a wood, doused with petrol and set alight as McNeilly chanted: 'Burn, baby, burn.' She survived for four days. The Judge, Mr Justice Potts, said: 'It was as appalling a murder as it is possible to imagine.'

After the wedding McNeilly wrote to a friend: 'I felt a bit daft in all that gear but Ma is well worth it and it was her special day. She's a proper lady. Ma looked the bizz. Honest it was beautiful, Unchained Melody playing as she walked down the aisle in the chapel with me. I was crying, nearly had to choke 'em back. Ha, ha!'

Linda's account continues:

It was agreed that any staff who wanted to attend would be allowed to be there and about thirty of them accepted invitations. Mr Smith had just retired but he agreed to return to take the wedding pictures.

At the last minute Governor Mitchell left and was replaced by a horrible man called Governor Daly who immediately began to disrupt the wedding plans. I heard that staff who were off duty but intended to come in to attend the wedding were told that they would be barred from entering the prison that day.

He even asked Mr Smith not to come and take the photos, and when that failed he confiscated the films and sent them to the police for, he said, intelligence purposes. That backfired because the police charged the prison for the cost of developing and printing – a total of £400.

We were the first couple that had ever been married in Durham Prison chapel which is over 100 years old. The service was brilliant. They were doing renovations on the jail at the time, but the driver of the cement-mixer lorry which was working outside the chapel had to turn his engine off so that everyone could hear the service. We did laugh. Considering it was a prison wedding, it was pretty good. We were allowed guests in from 10 o'clock in the morning and it went through until 4 o'clock in the afternoon.

Danny was brought across from the Category A wing and we all went across from the H block. After the service the governor got on the radio and ordered Danny to be handcuffed to go across to the H block where the reception was being held, but the head of security defied him. 'No. I'm not putting handcuffs on him,' he said. 'He's just got married. He can walk back and hold his wife's hand.'

* * *

Danny Reece's recollections of his courtship and marriage are altogether more prosaic and go back to the moment in Brixton Prison when he first saw Linda Calvey. He recalls:

Linda was visiting Brian Thorogood and my mum was visiting me. The first time I saw her she was wearing a fur coat which she removed before sitting down. I looked at her. She looked at me. And our eyes locked. After that I began writing to Linda regularly. I felt we had a genuine platonic friendship – a friendship whereby you can tell the other person anything. I could talk to her about all my problems and she would listen without judging me.

When it came to our trial for murder I didn't think, in my wildest dreams, that I would be found guilty. When we were both convicted I felt it was me and Linda against the world. I looked at her and in that moment all the feelings that were deep inside me came to the surface. I remembered the moment when I first set eyes on her. How our eyes had locked. It was the most startling thing that has ever happened to me. She is the most magnificent person I have ever met. She is beautiful.

When it came to our marriage in Durham, although the ceremony was in prison, for me the surroundings didn't exist. It was our special time as we made our vows to each other.

Linda's love has been the only thing that has kept me alive. The death of my son John had assumed massive importance in my mind. It was way out of proportion. Struggling with it has taken me to the brink of death many times, but Linda's love brought me back. I will never stop loving her. I worship her. I have lain in bed and experienced telepathy. Our thoughts have transferred. We have written letters on the same day and each received the letters containing identical thoughts. We are so in tune with one another that we couldn't be more in tune if we were twins. What goes on between us is a power so strong that it could light up the world.

The cruellest blow is being kept apart from Linda. It seems the authorities have done it deliberately. The law states that we can see each other every ninety days, but we have spent nine months apart.

I hope we will be released soon because I would like to have some input into my sons' lives before I am too old.

My future is with Linda. Every day and every night I think of her and I write every day. I am able to speak to her every fortnight. If I am lucky I get an hour but sometimes it is only ten minutes.

I have learned to control my rage by doing press-ups and have broken two world records, but I don't sleep well and I will never obtain peace of mind until I am reunited with Linda who tells me she is looking forward to the day when she can pamper me.

I've never been pampered. I can't wait.

11

MY FRIENDS IN THE NICK

L inda Calvey has now spent fourteen of her fifty-three years
behind bars – a chastening experience, undoubtedly, but also
an opportunity to observe the human condition from a different
perspective and establish unique and binding friendships. Linda,
being Linda, has her own special view on life behind the prison
walls:

Even after all these years I still can't believe that I'm sitting in
prison with a life sentence. I know that Ron must have turned in his
grave when he heard what was said in court about me.

At that time, if you came back to Holloway Prison with a life
sentence they put you on the hospital wing, which was the most
dreadful place, full of people who were desperate mental cases. I
was perfectly normal but, sure enough, that was where they put me

167

and for someone like me – a fighter and an active individual – that was the last place I needed to be under the circumstances.

The day after my conviction I saw the prison doctor who wanted to put me on Valium to help me cope with the idea of a life sentence. I said: 'Listen, if you give me Valium for a week, in a week's time I will still have this life sentence. I don't want Valium. I don't take medication. I don't want sleeping tablets. I can sleep. I need my mind active and clear to fight for my freedom. To win my appeal.' I had to assure him that I wasn't in a state of terminal depression – that I wasn't going to slash my wrists or try to hang myself.

The following day he relented and sent me back to a normal wing where I began the long hard slog of trying to prove my innocence.

It took a year to get to the Appeal Court and we had high hopes. We sat in the court and expected to walk free. Even the screws who were with us were convinced that we had won the appeal.

Sadly, even though the judges declared that there were weaknesses in the evidence which had convicted us, we had nothing new to present to them beyond the case originally given to the jury.

When the appeal was turned down was the first time I felt despair. I just kept thinking 'My God, when is this nightmare going to end?'

Something quite bizarre and probably unprecedented happened that day. One of the prison officers who was convinced of my innocence had volunteered to come in on her day off to escort me to the Appeal Court for the hearing, just to have the pleasure of being with me when I walked free. When we lost she was very sweet to me and allowed me some time with Danny before the prison van came to take him back to prison on the Isle of Wight. After a while, an official at the Appeal Court came in and said that the van coming to collect me was going to be delayed by over an hour and, since he wanted to go home, we would have to wait outside. Why is it that extraordinary things always happen to me? I had gone to court expecting to have my life sentence overturned, been told that I was still a life prisoner and a couple of hours later found myself turfed out on the street anyway!

It was so weird. There was a young male trainee prison officer with us and he was in a panic. He wanted to handcuff me, but the friendly female officer assured him that I would not misbehave. So the three of us sat on a bench outside the court, waiting for the prison van, while the people of London walked by oblivious to the fact I was a lifer.

I have never heard of anything like it before or since. You wouldn't even allow a person who was doing a couple of months for shoplifting to sit outside the court like that. I had a life sentence for murder and was being told to go and wait on the pavement.

I had been so sure that I was going home that I had given away everything I owned in Holloway – my radio, flask, all my clothes – to the other inmates. I was just going to walk out of the court in the clothes I was wearing. When I came back the whole wing was deserted. Nobody knew what to say to me. They felt awkward about seeing me. All the girls had gone back into their cells and the officers into their rooms. In my cell all my belongings had been returned and put back on the bed. I had to go out and find everybody and assure them that I was not giving up, that I could cope, and they could speak to me. So many of the girls and even staff cried for me on that day.

After my conviction for murder I should have been made a Category A prisoner – the category reserved for the most dangerous, unruly inmates and those most likely to escape. There are very few Cat A prisoners among the women in the British prison system, so there is just one high-security cell block for them and that is at Durham Prison. However, during the year I was awaiting my appeal, due to an administrative error at the Home Office, I was not classified as Category A which I should have been, due to the fact that I was seen as such a dangerous murderess!

At the time I was being moved between Holloway and Bullwood

Hall Prison in Essex. So, when the civil servants discovered their oversight, they created a special category for me – a 'Travelling Category A' – which meant that I was treated as a normal prisoner inside the jail, but subject to maximum security when I was outside the prison walls being transported anywhere or appearing in a court.

It was while I was at Holloway that I first met Rosemary Aberdour, the notorious Lady R who had swindled a charity out of £3 million and run off to Rio. Her future husband went to Brazil and brought her back and she was sent to Holloway. On her first morning I spotted her in the exercise yard with women inmates gathering round her like a flock of vultures waiting to pounce on their prey. I thought to myself: 'They're going to fleece her something rotten. I'll have to go and wise her up.' So I spoke to her, put her wise to the ways of Holloway and got her transferred to my wing so that she could be a wing cleaner with me.

After that we became very good friends. In fact, she later came to my wedding in Durham Prison and bought me a beautiful set of silk La Perla underwear to wear under my wedding dress. I appreciated that very much. She was a very genuine and nice person.

Several prison service observers were intrigued by the close relationship which developed between Linda Calvey and Rosemary Aberdour because they were both such different characters. Aberdour said she would always be grateful to Calvey for helping her through her jail ordeal. At first she compared Holloway to a girls' public school and said she was well treated by the warders, but later she complained that she was sexually harassed.

The pair had much in common when it came to a love of the high life. When Rosemary Aberdour lived it up she did it in style. She bought herself a Bentley turbo car worth £50,000 and hired a chauffeur to go with it. In the course of a few years she splashed out an amazing £780,000 on parties, once setting up an entire funfair in London's docklands. She bought a string of luxury cars, including a Mercedes and five other smaller models for her staff at a cost of over £200,000, and in one lavish week poured 240 bottles of Dom Perignon champagne into a bath for a friend to bathe in. There were Caribbean yachting holidays, buying trips to London jewellers and clothes purchased from the best couturiers in London and Paris.

But 'Lady' Aberdour was a fake – a suburban girl who swindled almost £3 million from a hospital charity before she was caught. Her fiancé, Army helicopter pilot Michael Cubbin, shared her lifestyle but claimed he was taken in by her aristocratic airs. He was questioned and cleared of involvement in her frauds, and stood by her throughout her trial and conviction.

Linda Calvey, the great prison correspondent, was instrumental in Aberdour striking up a prison friendship with another murderer. She persuaded Rosemary to become a penpal of Graham Backhouse, who tried to murder his wife in a car bomb attack because he wanted a £100,000 insurance payout. He then killed neighbour Colyn Bedale-Taylor, claiming it was self-defence. Backhouse, who died of a heart attack in prison, became obsessed with Rosemary. After she was released on parole, she was able to set up the lucrative knitwear company which funds her lifestyle now that she is a free woman.

Rosemary Aberdour was not Linda Calvey's only high-profile friend behind bars:

Another one of my prison friends was Reg Kray. He was a lovely man and I got on very, very well with him. I first met him when I was in my twenties and just married. We used to go down to the clubs owned by the Kray twins in the East End because they both knew my Micky.

Both Ron and Reg were delightful in the way they behaved towards women. I can't say what they were like to men, although I know their reputation, but they were very gentlemanly in their dealings with women.

Reg wrote to me when I was first in Durham Prison and I replied. After that we used to speak on the phone every week. Reg also proposed marriage to me. It was funny. I turned him down and told him that I was asking Danny, and then Danny turned me down.

Typically, when I told Reg that I had been turned down by Danny he said: 'Linda, if something is worth having then pursue it.' I'm so glad that I took his advice and kept going until Danny finally relented.

Reggie used to send me big bouquets of flowers, perfume and sports clothes, and even sent presents to some of the other girls when I mentioned that I was concerned about them.

One day I got a big bouquet of long-stemmed white roses from Reg, but as they were delivered I was in a hurry because I was going off to meet some visitors in the visiting hall. One of the girls, June Leaning, said: 'Stand them in a bucket and I'll watch them for you 'til you return.' Well, she was one of the inmates whose behaviour was unpredictable. Sometimes I thought I was living in a mental asylum in Durham, but on this occasion I thought it was unlikely that she could mess up a simple job like standing flowers in a bucket, so I agreed.

When I came back from the visit I looked up the stairs and all I could see was stalks sticking out of the top of the bucket and I thought: 'Oh, for God's sake! She's put them in the bucket upside down.' But when I got upstairs, I discovered that she'd snapped all the heads off and spread them around the table.

The next day, when Reg rang to ask if I'd received the roses all right, I told him the story. 'I think she's one of the nutters,' I said.

Reggie just roared with laughter. 'Too right!' he said. 'Anybody who'd do that to a bouquet with "From Reg Kray" written on it must be mad!'

The next day I got another bouquet to replace the mangled one. That's what Reg was like. He was so sweet. He really had a heart of gold. He was always doing things to help other people. On several occasions he painted me pictures, when members of staff were trying to raise money for charity through raffles. On another occasion, one of the staff told me that her daughter who hero-worshipped Reg was very ill and had to go into hospital for an operation. Reg sent her an autographed book and several little presents.

It is so sad that he was not shown the same compassion that he gave out, so tragic that in the end he just went home to die and not home to live. It is heartbreaking to me that both Ronnie and Reggie died the way they did and never had the chance to live a proper life outside the prison walls.

Talking earlier of mentally disturbed prisoners reminds me of the truly sad part of British prison life. The whole of the British prison system is chock-a-block with people who should not be in jail. They should be in mental hospitals and institutions for the mentally deficient. These people may have committed crimes due to their mental condition, but they mostly did not know what they were doing, and instead of punishment they need treatment. It is almost as if the prisons have become society's dumping grounds for these pathetic creatures who nobody wants so it is easier to lock them away out of sight.

For the staff and the other inmates the presence of these people can be very distressing and at times traumatising.

In Holloway, for instance, C1 Wing was the infamous wing for the mentally disturbed, where the staff had to walk down the centre of the corridor to avoid the grasping hands being thrust through the bars to grab them.

I have noticed that it is typical of the mentally ill, where they are gathered together in a group, that if one does something they all follow suit.

While I was in Holloway, I shared a dormitory with a girl called

Linda who was given the duty of cleaning on C1 Wing. Mostly her duties provided us with a good deal of amusement. It was routine for her to have just finished cleaning the floor when one of the girls would yell: 'I'm throwing my cup of tea out of the hatch,' followed by a cascade of cups clattering to the floor all along the corridor and a fresh mess to clean up.

One day Linda returned ashen-faced from her cleaning duties with a most distressing story to tell. Apparently one of the mentally disturbed inmates on a deranged whim had called out: 'I'm pulling my eye out,' and had ripped her eyeball from its socket – not just on to her cheek but right out of her head – and thrown it out of the hatch.

Immediately the girl next door yelled: 'I'm ripping my eye out,' followed by a chorus of similarly wild commitments from the others on the wing.

A quick-thinking prison officer immediately raced along the corridor shouting: 'No, no, it's a joke, she hasn't done it. It's just a laugh.' As she ran she forced herself to laugh and soon all the disturbed inmates were giggling helplessly and the crisis had passed.

The prison nurse, who was quickly on the scene, took a tissue from her pocket, bent down and picked the eye up. When Linda remonstrated with her about hygiene she simply said: 'It doesn't matter anymore. This eyeball can't be put back in.'

That episode affected us all very deeply for several days.

Another girl cut her nipples off and flushed them down the toilet. What are these people doing in prison?

There was another tiny little pretty girl, on remand, who killed herself on the eve of her court appearance by somehow managing to turn her metal bed up on end, without anyone in the dormitory hearing, and hanging herself with her nightie from the metal headboard. Just tragic. I've seen so much of it over the years.

Talking of prison suicides, one of the most shocking events I can remember happened on a Saturday morning in Durham. One of the girls, Jeanie, who was just starting a life sentence with a long tariff for a particularly nasty crime, was found unconscious in her cell at breakfast time. She had swallowed all her medication and a large amount of sleeping tablets all at once. She was as good as dead – but not quite. Staff telephoned to the hospital and a nursing sister came over. She went into the cell while we all stood around gawping. After a matter of seconds she came out and shut the cell door.

The Principal Officer, Mr Atkins, stepped forward and asked: 'What's the situation?'

'She's nearly dead,' replied the nurse.

'What do you mean *nearly* dead?' he inquired. 'She's either dead or she's alive.'

Mr Atkins saved Jeanie's life by ordering an ambulance immediately.

Jeanie recovered and the last time I was in Durham she was still there, so her death can't have been meant can it?

In Durham I met two of the best governors I've come across in the system, Governor John Smith and Governor Micky Martin, and I'm sure it is no coincidence that they both started out as physical training instructors and worked their way up through the ranks. They were both humane men with a genuine concern for the inmates and an innate ability to understand what made us all tick.

Prison Officer Usher, head of security, also deserves a mention for the way he helped to make my wedding to Danny so special against serious opposition from many other members of staff.

Two of my long-serving fellow inmates are two of the women most hated by the outside world – Myra Hindley and Rose West.

Myra has suffered a good deal of ill-health in recent years, in particular the brittle bone disease which still plagues her.

The first time that became apparent was when we were all sitting outside in the exercise yard at Durham on a particularly sunny afternoon. An officer looked out and shouted: 'Come on girls, inside now.' I've no idea why the order came in that way at that time because there didn't seem any urgency for us all to go back to our cells, but it made us all hurry up. Myra was sitting cross-legged on the ground and she went to lever herself up to a standing position, but when her bottom was no more than about nine inches off the ground her hand slipped on the grass and she plopped back down. At that there were two audible cracks and Myra cried out in pain. She had fractured her leg very badly in two places.

They sent for an ambulance for Myra, but while it was on its way they discovered that one of the other lifers had taken an overdose. So they sent her off in that ambulance and left Myra lying on the ground in the exercise yard. One of the officers said: 'She can't go anywhere can she? The weather's nice and sunny, just leave her there.'

She had surgery to put in all sorts of metal pins and plates and her leg still plays her up to this day. Only last year she had to have further surgery because one of the pins from one of the plates had worked free and had been digging into a nerve for years, so she had that replaced to remove the constant pain.

In fact the press were misinformed about the reason for Myra Hindley's fracture which happened on 14 April 1995. The *Daily Mirror* reported:

> Moors murderess Myra Hindley was said to be in agony last night after breaking a leg in a jail keep-fit session.
>
> Hindley, 52, is believed to have become obsessed with keeping her weight down as she serves a life sentence for child killings.
>
> In a vigorous work-out at Durham Prison on Friday she fell snapping a thigh bone. An insider said: 'The fracture is severe. She is in absolute agony.'
>
> Angina sufferer Hindley was taken under heavy police escort to Durham's Dryburn hospital for the fracture to be

pinned. She was put in a single room with two women prison guards as medical staff prepared for her surgery.

The child killer, given life in 1966, was moved to Durham jail from Cookham Wood in Kent last month.

Hindley returned to the prison after a five-day stay in hospital, but the matter was to plunge the prison service into controversy the following year when the former inspector of Prisons, Judge Stephen Tumim clashed with Durham's hard-line governor over more 'humane' treatment for Hindley.

Relatives of Hindley's victims were incensed when Judge Tumim suggested that the child-killer be allowed to decide how she led life in prison and be given a suitable occupation, a computer and better access to telephones. Instead the newly installed Durham governor, Niall Clifford, ordered Hindley back to the high-security H Wing. She had spent four months in comparative luxury in the hospital wing recovering from her broken leg, but was forced back to spending ten hours a day in her cell.

The whole controversy blew up exactly thirty years to the day after Hindley and her lover Ian Brady were convicted of murdering Lesley Ann Downey, and ten, and seventeen-year-old Edward Evans. Brady was convicted of killing twelve-year-old John Kilbride. Hindley later confessed that they had also killed Pauline Reade, who was sixteen and twelve-year-old Keith Bennett. She has been told that she will never be released. She will die in prison.

Before her move to Durham, she had been held at Cookham Wood where privileges such as unsupervised walks and private visits prompted warders to complain to the governor of 'appeasement'.

Actually, although Linda claims a warm friendship with both Myra Hindley and Rose West, the prison authorities seem to think otherwise and have, on occasion, taken urgent steps to prevent her harming each of the two most notorious female prisoners in the British prison system.

In May 1996 she was hurriedly moved out of Durham's H Wing for a 28-day cooling off period after a row and threats which led the governor to believe that she was poised to attack Rose West.

Last autumn her wing was closed down for several hours while prison officers attached to the security section conducted a cell search for weapons with which it was alleged that Linda intended to attack Myra Hindley. They reputedly confiscated a crudely made knife, but Linda denies all knowledge of this and insists that the raids were carried out on bogus information planted by other inmates determined to cause trouble for her.

Linda's daily life in Durham was rarely without incident as she explains:

Durham contains a number of women convicted of arson and it is a psychological condition which apparently never leaves them. Two Christmases ago I went back up to Durham to visit Danny and while I was there, there was a spate of cell fires set by these arsonists. One of the cells which was torched was Rose West's.

Her pride and joy is a budgerigar which was in the room at the time it was set on fire. The staff managed to rescue the poor little bird, but it was barely recognisable because of the smoke and soot which had blackened and singed its feathers. Rose went into such a decline over the state of the bird that she went to bed for two days and refused to come out.

There was a real irony in her hysteria. Rose is the only person I've ever seen in my life literally to foam at the mouth through anger. When she discovered the plight of her pet, she began to scream and rage: 'How could anybody be that wicked and evil to set a fire and leave a bird to die?' I just thought to myself: ' "How could anybody be that wicked and evil?" And this from Rose West who is doing so many life sentences for murder including her own children?'

But she was adamant: 'I've never heard of anything so cruel. How could anyone do such a thing?' she stormed.

My friend Sue May, who is also doing life for murder, was given the job of bathing the budgie. It was hilarious because she was paranoid that the bird would drop dead with shock over the bathing and she'd be blamed for its death. I think she had to clean it about four times to get all the soot off. It was extraordinary to see all these murderesses in such a state over the life or death of a budgie.

The arsonists were actually a real pain to all of us.

Durham had been without any proper hairdressing facilities for years, until the governor decided to set aside a room for a salon and donate some money for equipment. A whole rank of brand new hairdryers and every piece of equipment you could think of for a beauty salon were supplied and fitted. It was a real boost to morale for all the girls.

Then, within weeks of it opening, somebody set the salon on fire.

We were all furious because, between the flames and the firemen's water, everything was destroyed.

So Prison Officer Atkins, who was such a nice man, got us all together and he said: 'Now, come on girls. Somebody knows what happened here and somebody knows who did it. Perhaps somebody would like to come and speak to me in private.'

We all just stood there, looking sullenly at each other, when one inmate, June Leaning, who was in jail for arson, all of a sudden blurted out: 'I saved a pair of curling tongs.'

'Did you, June,' said Mr Atkins. 'And when did you save them?'

'Before the fire started,' she said.

'How did you know there was going to be a fire?' he asked and we all just went mad. We all now knew it was her that had set the fire.

My first recollection of June, just after I arrived at Durham and knew no one, was when she approached me for help. She is a frail-looking elderly lady and she told me confidentially that she was having a problem with arsonists.

'I'm frightened to leave my room, because every time I go out somebody comes in and tries to set it on fire,' she said, 'so would you do me a favour and sit outside my door while I nip downstairs for something?'

I agreed and dutifully sat on a chair outside her room for five minutes until she returned and thanked me.

As I turned to leave she pushed the door open and screamed: 'Somebody's done it again. My room's on fire.'

Sure enough, quite a little blaze had taken hold in the room. While she had been away nobody had passed me, but in my panic I overlooked the obvious and just began yelling for help to put the fire out. It was only when help arrived that it became clear that she had stuffed toilet paper all over the room and set it alight before tricking me into sitting guard over her handiwork.

I did have a red face after that and was never caught out by the arsonists again.

June Leaning became notorious as the babysitter who was hailed as a heroine after failing in a brave attempt to rescue two children from a house fire – which she had started herself.

She battled in vain through thick smoke to reach the youngsters, attended their funeral and gave evidence at the inquest into their deaths, but the fifty-year-old housewife was given two life sentences in 1992 after pleading guilty to manslaughter and five counts of arson.

Nottingham Crown Court heard that she was regarded by her neighbours as a 'kindly, maternal person who was fond of children'. In fact she was a pyromaniac who had started three previous fires. Two similar incidents had occurred when she was babysitting in the year prior to the deaths, but no one was injured. She also started a fire at her husband's parents' house and then returned to her own home to watch television. Her father-in-law was almost overcome by smoke from the blaze.

David Farrer QC for the prosecution said: 'To her neighbours, she appeared to be the least likely source of such a tragedy, but she had a compulsive fascination for lighting fires and for their consequences. She told police she was excited at seeing the fire brigade arrive. She is a very dangerous woman.'

The two children died after she set fire to sheets in the airing cupboard with a cigarette. The court heard that 'she saw the flames rising and she closed the door . . . with the fire burning and the children asleep in a nearby bedroom'. She went downstairs to watch television with her husband who made her a cup of tea. She helped neighbours in a failed rescue attempt and the children died of asphyxia. The cause of the fire was recorded as an electrical fault.

Mr Farrer said that Mrs Leaning was of limited intelligence and mentally ill. 'The motive seems to have been the excitement of provoking this kind of disturbance and being, for the time, part of the focus of that disturbance,' he said.

Her defence counsel, Graham Buchanan, said she was a caring woman who had no motive for wishing the children ill and appeared deeply upset by the deaths. 'She is suffering from an illness, a sickness . . . in respect of which there appears to be no medical treatment,' he said. 'She is not evil in the normally accepted sense.'

In the year after the deaths of five-year-old Simon Graham and his two-year-old sister Lucy in May 1989, June Leaning started two more fires and plagued the fire brigade with hoax calls on the estate in Barton, near Grimsby where she lived. She was finally reported to the police when neighbours caught her starting a fire in the porch of a house in her street.

Linda's account continues:

There weren't only nutters in Durham, there were some extraordinary people too.

Politics aside, I have to say that the two women I most admired for sheer strength of character were Martina Anderson and Ella

O'Dwyer, the two IRA terrorists who bombed Margaret Thatcher's cabinet at the Brighton conference. When I went to Durham, they had been in prison for ten years already, but they were such fit, healthy, mentally tough and attractive well-dressed women that I was in awe of them. They had been in that horrible dump for so many years and yet they looked like visitors who had just walked in there for the day – mentally alert and bright – and they never lost their spirit.

I don't believe in terrorism in any shape or form – I reject the whole idea – but I admired their strength. Had it not been for the Irish peace process, they would still have another ten or fifteen years to do. When they left, H-block was never the same again. They had fought so hard to get concessions for the girls in there, but gradually things they had fought for were removed. The last time I was there it had slipped back.

There are lighter moments in prison, though. I remember an incident, while we were all queuing for food in the dining hall in Holloway, when two of the girls began arguing over a piece of chicken. Several bowls of soapy water always left on the counter for girls to put their dirty plates in when they'd finished eating. On this occasion the argument escalated to the point where one of the girls picked up a bowl of soapy water and tipped it over the head of the other. The second girl immediately hurled her plate of fruit cocktail, jelly and custard, which missed her attacker and landed on the back of my head, much to the dismay of one of the nutters standing behind me. By now the alarm bell had sounded and prison officers began to rush into the dining hall. The first one skidded on the soapy water and flew, flat on her back, across the floor, upsetting tables, chairs, and food as she went. The others tumbled in on top of her in a heap. It was like a scene from a *Carry On* film. Hilarious.

Hygiene was not at the highest level in Holloway in those days. I remember lying in bed in our dormitory one evening, chatting to

Linda the cleaner from C1 Wing. She was in the bed opposite leaning up against the wall. My friend Ashley and I sat without saying a word as we watched a cockroach walk up the wall and go into her hair. She leapt out of bed cursing us for not warning her and we just fell about laughing. The alarming thing, looking back on it, was that cockroaches were so commonplace that we had watched it walk up, knowing it was heading for Linda's head, without any reaction.

In fact the infestation at Holloway is so severe that they will never get rid of the vermin. There are detailed coloured posters all over the place, identifying the types of cockroaches and which parts of the world they come from. Can you imagine tolerating those sort of living conditions in your own home?

It is extraordinary to me to think that security in prisons has been stepped up since the Irish peace process and the release of all the terrorist prisoners when it was so lax up until that time. I remember an incident once when Kate came to visit me in Durham and, as usual, was able to bring her handbag in without anybody checking it. Ronnie Kray, her husband, was very concerned about her security at the time and had bought her a stun gun for her protection. He insisted she carry it at all times. Kate forgot the gun was at the bottom of her bag and was unaware that she'd brought it into the prison. There it was. A stun gun in her handbag being brought in unchecked to supposedly one of Britain's most secure jails!

The women's visiting room at Durham is quite tiny – just three tables and curtains are drawn so that you and your visitors can have privacy. On this particular day the only other people in there apart from me and Kate were the two IRA girls and their husbands. Ella's husband had been released and was living at home in Ireland, but he'd come over for the day, and Martina's husband, who was also doing time, was on an inter-prison visit. It was all a mistake because they were not supposed to see their husbands at the same time, so both men were asked not to communicate with one another during the visit.

Things have been tightened up over the years, so that some of the things I used to do could not happen these days.

There was a time in Holloway, for instance, when we were allowed to have children in on visits – either your children or grandchildren. In my case it was my eldest grand-daughter Sammy. It was lovely.

At that time the visitor was allowed to bring in food for you and the child. They still do children's visits, but they've stopped the food. I used to have two big hold-alls brought in for these visits, filled with Marks & Spencer's food – cakes, prawns, salads, fruit gateaux, chicken, fancy cheeses, fruit juices and all the lovely ready meals. By no stretch of the imagination could one person have eaten all this food – it would have taken a week and still there would have been some left over.

I had an arrangement with my friend Sonia Martin who was a wing cleaner with me. She used to make an excuse to take the wing washing down to the laundry when I was visiting with Sammy. Then she would pop in, ostensibly to see Sammy, and take the food back up to the wing in the laundry bag. Our room used to feast for days. Marks & Spencer's delicacies used to taste brilliant after prison food. When the doors were locked and all the food came out, we used to toast each other in fruit juice and take on airs and graces like ladies. The food tasted even better because it was our little bit of defiance and a small victory over prison rules.

Similarly, years ago, when I was in East Sutton Park open prison telephones for prisoners were a new thing. These days you can only use special prison phone cards, so that prisoners can be rationed in the number of calls they make and the number of cards they have. However, in those days my friend Pam and I, when we went out to work in the nearby town, brought back loads of phone cards because they worked in the phones in the prison and we did a roaring trade with the other girls. Again it was a little bit of defiance which made us feel better.

These little moments of beating the system are very important to inmates.

At one time, years ago, Micky was in Chelmsford prison in Essex and the control over visitors was fairly lax. Visitors had to wait in an area in the centre of the prison where there was a toilet with a cleaning cupboard in it. One day Micky slipped me a cuttle fish with the impression of the cupboard key in it and gave me the name of a friend who was going to make a key from the impression. On the next visit I had to check that the key worked, which it did. There was nothing in the cupboard, so after that I would fill my bags with what appeared to be shopping. I used to take drink into the prison and lock it in the cupboard with some nice food which the prisoner who was on cleaning duty would collect for them all to have at the weekends.

Micky came up with the idea of me blowing up balloons while I was in the toilet and putting them in my shopping bag to fill them out and make them look as full as when I'd come into the prison. I was always terrified that the wind would blow as I was leaving and expose the scam.

That went on for years until Micky was transferred, and years later he said to me: 'The best drop of drink I've ever had in my life was what you brought in because it was drink we shouldn't have had and it was one up to us.' I could never understand that, until I was in the same position.

The apparently lax regimes enjoyed by some prisoners serving long sentences for serious crimes is a constant source of anger and dismay for some sections of the media. Linda's notoriety as a gangster and murderess has often thrust her to the forefront of such censorious publicity.

In February 1998, the *Mail on Sunday*, under the headline: 'Why was this strip show allowed in a British prison?' published a picture of a pretty girl leaping from a box, wearing only a black lace basque and stockings. In terms of righteous outrage the report ran:

It is a scene captured on camera at thousands of retirement parties in offices and factories every week. But these pictures are not simply a reminder of the day catering manager Gerry Cole left work. They also provide a damning snapshot of the degeneration of Britain's prison service.

For this sea of squealing, laughing faces contains some of the country's most notorious women criminals. Even the scantily clad kissagram is a heroin-addicted prostitute and drugs courier.

Astonishingly, the party, with its sausage rolls, sandwiches, and cake – topped with icing models of naked women – took place inside Holloway Prison. It was organised by the inmates and held away from prison officers or any other form of control.

At the centre of the celebration, carefully coiffed and dressed for the party are three women: Linda Calvey, the notorious Black Widow, Angela Dodge, who took two elderly sisters on a three-year fraud spree, and drugs courier Katherine Brooks.

12

THE FUTURE

From the moment of her conviction Linda Calvey has quietly but firmly campaigned for justice for herself and all other lifers. From behind bars she still keeps pressure on the authorities to change the law which allows prisoners serving life sentences to be kept locked up indefinitely if they refuse to admit their guilt.

Ten years ago, while held in Bullwood Hall Prison in Essex, she led a group of ten female lifers in writing a letter to the *Independent* newspaper which read:

Sir: Lifers are the only inmates who do not have a set date for release; a tariff is given, but we are all made uncomfortably aware that not only are we expected to serve it, but that we could serve longer, our sentence being decided not by a judge in a court of law, but by a civil servant in the Home Office.

To be considered for release, a lifer must satisfy certain conditions. One of these is that we accept and admit our guilt for the crime for which we have been convicted and sentenced. In view of the disturbing number of recent miscarriages of justice that are coming to light in the Court of Appeal, this policy can only compound the errors of a seriously flawed system and cause misery to those who are its victims.

The Home Secretary must seek to abolish the mandatory life sentence in order to serve the best interests of the public and those in custody.

Despite losing her appeal against conviction, to her apparent amazement, and having her first parole application turned down last year, Linda remains adamant about her innocence in relation to Ronnie Cook's killing. Her letters and conversations are peppered with optimistic references to the future – a future, as she sees it, of happiness and contentment with her children and grandchildren, secure in the knowledge that her name has been cleared.

She holds to the original story she told the police, that a mystery gunman, dressed all in black, burst into her house and shot Cook twice in front of her before fleeing the murder scene.

The motive for the murder, she hints, was fear. Cook, while in prison, had sworn deadly vengeance on at least two people he blamed for his capture and incarceration. He had vast criminal wealth salted away, which he suspected was being wasted or even stolen by people he had trusted to manage it for him. His presence back on the streets, a free man, threatened not only the lives of these people, but the nefarious livelihoods of other criminal gangs who had moved into the vacuum left in the underworld while he was in jail. She has no idea who it might have been.

Linda repeatedly rebuts any suggestion that she had fallen out of love with Cook or that she was not prepared to have him back or to set up home with him when he was freed.

Recently Linda's defence was given an unexpected boost by a bizarre and quite sensational new confession from her co-defendant Danny Reece.

The killing took place in Calvey's home in King George Avenue, Plaistow on the afternoon of Monday 19 November 1990. Both the prosecution and defence case revolve around the events of that weekend which began when Linda and her friend Ashley Fitts picked up Danny Reece from the Verne Prison in Portland, Dorset, on the morning of Friday 16 November.

This is Linda's explanation for some of the events of that weekend which were later used in evidence against her:

Ronnie and I had got into quite a routine of coming home on the Mondays and Wednesdays. I used to pick him up from Maidstone and bring him to my house and make him a drink. Then we'd go straight upstairs to bed. Afterwards, I would cook him a bit of dinner and take him back again. Sweet! We both looked forward to it.

This particular week I saw him on the Wednesday and we agreed to see each other as usual on the following Monday.

On the Friday I'd picked up Danny Reece for his weekend leave and he'd had dinner at my house that evening with Ashley and me.

On the Sunday I was over at Ashley's and we'd just got back from buying shellfish for tea from Chapel Market when the phone rang. It was Ron. He was in The Widow's Son, the pub run by his nephew Paul and his wife Sylvie. They'd picked him up from Maidstone that morning. He was quite merry and insisting that I go down and have a drink with him. When you've been away a long time, you don't need much alcohol to make you drunk.

It was busy in the pub, being Sunday lunchtime. I managed to get a parking space in the little car park and as I walked in half-noticed somebody who was sitting outside with a white baseball cap on. If I thought anything about it I imagine I just thought the person was outside because they must have had too much to drink.

At court later they tried to say that this individual with the white baseball cap – the same as the killer wore – was Danny, sitting watching to have me identify Ron to him. But that was the first time I'd ever had a drink with Ron at The Widow's Son, so I'd have had to have been a clairvoyant to know that he was going to be there that day and tip off Danny.

As I walked in, Ron was standing talking to a couple of people at the end of the bar. He said, 'Hello, Sweetheart', put his arm around me and gave me a big kiss. We then had a public conversation about who was going to take him back to prison that night, and the fact that I was picking him up to bring him to my home the following day, the Monday, was mentioned within earshot of several people.

I am convinced that is how the gunman who shot him got to know where he would be the next day.

Ron was a bit tipsy and asked if we could sit down. In court it was suggested that I had lured him to sit at a table where Danny could get a good look at him – evidence was given that he frequently used to visit the pub with his wife and always stood at the bar, never sat down. My defence pointed out that men are frequently more attentive to their lovers than their wives and it would not be unusual for him to have sat down alone with me. Actually, if you wanted a good view of Ron from outside, you only had to open the pub door because he was standing with me directly in line with it.

Also, why would a contract killer need to identify the target, when all he needed to know was that the target was the only person walking into my house alone with me at the agreed time?

I recall a typical conversation in the pub that afternoon when Paul took a break from serving at the bar and wandered over to join us. We had been discussing Ron's imminent release and what he was going to buy me for Christmas. I wanted a Mercedes sports car – not red – and Ron had agreed.

I added: 'What about my "I waited for you present?" '

Ron burst out laughing. 'Don't you love her cheek?' he asked turning to Paul.

'What is it you wanted?' he asked me.

'I want a three-carat diamond ring, but I want a perfect stone, not a crappy one with bits in it,' I said.

'She's brilliant, isn't she'? Ron said to Paul, as he kissed me. 'We better get that sorted for Christmas.'

With that, Paul, who obviously didn't love my cheek or agree that I was brilliant, made an excuse and left. He clearly didn't approve of such extravagance.

After closing the pub, Paul invited us upstairs for dinner with him and his wife, but Ron told him that we'd rather spend time alone together down in the bar. When Paul had gone, he said to me: 'Does he really think I'd rather go up and have a dinner with him than make love to you? Come on.'

He took me out to the back of the bar where all the barrels were. The situation didn't allow for anything too passionate but we did make love there and then. Afterwards Ron said: 'I do love you, even though you've been a bastard to me.'

I said, 'No, you know that everything I've done you would've done yourself.' He agreed and chuckled. He was in a good mood.

One of the main prosecution planks during Calvey's trial was the suggestion that she had to murder Cook before he discovered that she had spent all his money. The expensive renovations to her house represented a key part of the evidence in support of this contention. Calvey said that Cook had authorised the use of the money and had ordered his 'banker' to pay for all the work out of funds he was managing for his imprisoned associate. However, according to Calvey, when he came to the witness box the man denied all knowledge of this and said that he had neither organised nor paid for the renovation work. This is Linda's version:

I told Ron all the things I wanted to have done to the house and he said: 'Whatever you want done, you have it done, and I'll get my man up here and tell him to pay for it.'

So I went with his friend on a visit and he seemed a bit reluctant, but Ron said to him, 'Listen, she's bought that home for me and her. I'm going to live there with her and I don't want any corners cut. Don't forget whose money you've got. Whatever she wants, she gets.'

The man was very sulky on the way home in the car and he asked: 'What is it you want?'

I just said: 'I want lots of things.'

So he sent some decorators round to do the whole job – exactly what I wanted – and I never paid them. He paid them as far as I know.

When I was coming to the end of my robbery sentence and I'd got parole, I always visited Ron twice on every home leave. I was picked up from prison on a Friday and I'd go to see him first, before I saw my family or my kids, and again on the Monday morning I'd see him early before I went back to prison.

In court, of course, the police were trying to say that I didn't want Ron anymore, but by then he'd been in prison ten years and my lawyers were able to produce the prison records. They showed that I'd been sent a visiting order every fortnight, and every fortnight I'd visited him, except when I was in prison myself, during which time I applied for and got regular inter-prison visits with him as my common-law husband. Why would I still be doing that if I didn't love him and want him back with me?

When I interviewed Danny two years ago he, too, swore that he was innocent, but his version of events was more vague and he had no real explanation for the confession he made to police when the attack on Ronnie Cook was first put to him. Several of his statements were inconsistent and begged a number of questions about his precise whereabouts during the course of that fateful weekend.

Speaking from his prison cell he said:

My son John was knocked down and killed while crossing the road. He was only sixteen. I couldn't seem to grasp it. It was too terrifying to accept.

I had been moved to a Category C prison and this entitled me to a home leave every three months. Linda visited me and she talked to me about the death of my son. She was very concerned about my feelings on his death. I had been unable to grieve for the boy because in my mind I still had not accepted it.

Linda made arrangements for us to go to the cemetery on my next home leave, to enable me to pay my respects and perhaps come to terms with the situation. She told me exactly where the grave was and insisted that I went to the graveside alone. My only recollection of that occasion was looking at the grave with John's name inscribed on the marble headstone, and the next thing I remember was sitting in the back of Linda's car.

She took me to my mum's house with the promise she would return later to take me to her home. All my brothers and sisters visited me and the hours flew by until the time when Linda came back to take me to her house for a huge dinner. I enjoyed that evening. Linda spoiled me by cooking a lovely meal and she had bought my favourite Shirley Bassey tape. I relaxed and forgot all thoughts of prison life.

Soon it was time to leave. Linda offered to drive me back, but I needed time to think so I made an excuse and left on my own. I went back to the cemetery and stayed at the side of John's grave all night. The next day I went back to Bracknell in Berkshire where we used to live and wandered around all John's favourite haunts –

places where I used to take him when he was a little kid.

I experienced a roller coaster of emotions that day. One minute up. The next minute down. When I felt angry I wanted to fight someone and went looking for a bloke who I knew would be my equal, but he was not there.

I borrowed a car for a few hours so that I could get around and see some friends. I managed to get through the day, avoiding trouble, and the next day, Sunday, I telephoned the owner to tell him where I had left the car and went back to London. I returned to the Verne Prison by train.

Two days later I telephoned home and was told that Ronnie Cook had been murdered. Within the week I was interviewed by the police and accused of doing it.

I did not have an alibi for my whereabouts on Friday night because I was alone in the cemetery. All of Saturday through to Sunday morning I was alone in Bracknell

I was moved to Winchester Prison and put on an identity parade. Needless to say I could not be identified. Then I was moved to Wandsworth Prison for a taped interview with the police. I was being accused of the murder of Ronnie Cook. I did not know the man personally. I didn't even know what he looked like. I had no reason to kill the man that Linda had been waiting years for.

The case was remanded for five weeks. Billy Francis, who was supposed to have been my getaway driver, was in the dock and the plot was thickening. The evidence was read out with the confessions. My confession was one I had apparently given when in the Verne Prison. Billy Francis's confession was dropped and he was let off all charges.

Two of the prosecution witnesses who were unable to identify me have positively identified another man as the killer. The description given at the time by reliable witnesses describes this man exactly. He was also responsible for the killing of Ronnie Cook's accountant and his girlfriend in Epping Forest.

My understanding is that he killed Ronnie over a drugs deal. Cook had invested £150,000 in the venture and been promised a healthy return on his money, but he was ripped-off and lost the lot. From inside prison he was issuing threats. You couldn't take Ronnie Cook's threats lightly. He was an extremely violent man when roused. He had to be killed first, before he exacted his own revenge.

This story about another killer was a reference to the notorious James Alfred Moody who escaped from Brixton Prison along with the IRA bomb-maker Gerard Tuite in 1980 and disappeared.

Moody was mysteriously murdered on 1 June 1993 while drinking in the bar of The Royal Hotel, Hackney, where he was known as Mick. He was shot dead by a man described as in his early forties and wearing a leather jacket. The man had ordered a pint of Foster's lager and put two coins down on the bar to pay for it. Then he moved towards Moody and fired three shots. As Moody slumped to the floor, a fourth shot was fired into his back before the killer was driven away in a stolen white Ford Fiesta XR2.

The motive for the execution remains unknown, but underworld sources persist in claiming that Moody was the hitman who carried out a number of contract killings including that of Terry Gooderham and his girlfriend Maxine Arnold, who were found shot dead in their black Mercedes in Epping Forest in 1989.

Gooderham had been a stocktaker for a number of clubs and pubs in London and Hertfordshire and may have had an association with Ronnie Cook. Among the many theories put forward for his murder was one that he was the victim of part of a drugs war and the killing was over £150,000 euphemistically described as having been 'redirected'.

The clear implication behind Reece's claim is that Moody was a hitman commissioned to kill Cook. All of this is conjecture, however, and flies in the face of the prosecution evidence.

Reece continued:

* * *

Linda and I have no doubt that this wrongful conviction will be overturned. Ronnie Cook's friends know who murdered him. His children want to believe that Linda was involved because their father loved Linda more than he loved their mother.

Linda would not have hurt a hair on his head. She was loyal to him as she is loyal to me.

So far, so good. The two killers maintain their innocence and offer explanations and motivations for others to be the culprits.

But then, last autumn, came an extraordinary twist to this most extraordinary of murder cases.

Danny Reece wrote a cryptic note to Linda, enclosing a letter he had received from Brian Thorogood whom he referred to as Gonzo. Addressing her as 'Soul Twin' he said he would be making a statement to her lawyers. He wrote that if, after she had read the statement, she wanted to have nothing more to do with him, he would understand and commit suicide to be with his son. Thorogood's letter turned out to be an apology and a confession that he had invented the stories about Ronnie Cook having tortured and brutalised Linda – stories which formed a major part of the prosecution case at the murder trial. The lies, he said, had been concocted to disgust and horrify Cook's friends, so that they would not carry out the retribution which Cook had sworn to exact on his former friend for stealing Linda's affections away from him. This deception, he hinted, had inadvertently become the root of all Danny's troubles and he felt responsible for Reece's murder conviction.

The statement Reece subsequently made to Linda's lawyers sparked off a fresh investigation into the murder of Ronnie Cook. In it he confessed to having carried out the killing because of his infatuation for Linda. He claimed to have believed the torture stories told by Thorogood, and in his rage determined to prevent Cook from ever getting his hands on the woman he loved again. He did not tell Linda because he was convinced that the prosecution would not succeed, or that they would both be freed on appeal. He insisted that he had lived with the guilt of taking the object of his love to prison with him for years, but had only decided to make his full confession after he had discovered Thorogood's deception.

While Linda and her lawyers were deciding what to do about Danny Reece's confession, he sent me a tape recording he had made in his cell at Whitemoor Prison in Cambridgeshire.

With the ambient sounds of prison life in the background and the distant noises of the Cambridgeshire countryside drifting in through the cell window, it is a rambling treatise which alternates between the pathetic and the downright hilarious. Sometimes he is almost incoherent as, complaining of a broken tooth, he lisps and curses his way through his story.

The two letters and the tape are fascinating and worthy of note, so I have reproduced them in their entirety. The sequence begins with Thorogood's letter which is undated.

Hello Danny,

As I said on the phone I would be writing you a letter. But believe me mate this is one letter I wish I did not have to write.

For years now I've had something on my mind and it is now driving me mad and I can no longer hold it in. It's to do with your life sentence and what you told me on a visit not so long ago as regards your sentence and Ronnie Cook.

Danny, it broke my heart as I feel so close to you and you have gone through so much. So here it is Danny, what I told you as regards what Ronnie Cook did to Linda (beatings, torture and so on) was all lies on my part.

I told everybody inside the same story that I told you.

The reason for this was simple. It was the only protection I could give myself against any of Cook's friends (and he had plenty) that I would meet on my last long sentence.

Once I told them the same lies I told you their answer was fuck him and I was well and truly left alone.

But of course I did not tell you for the same reasons but out of the friendship we had. How the fuck could I have ever guessed the outcome of those lies to you that was to come years later?

Danny, I am going to end this letter now as I've said all that I wanted to.

Anything else I will leave until a later date except just to say please try and find it in your heart to somehow forgive me.

God bless

Love

Your friend

Brian

Danny's letter to Linda, dated 6 October 2001 is as follows:

Reece N56981 Whitemoor

Longhill Road

March

Cambs

Soul Twin

I've enclosed this letter that I've received from Gonzo today. I know it will really confuse you baby and it will take me a phone then a letter to tell you what I've kept from you all this time.

So what I'm going to do is write a statement to your brief and when you get the copy you will know everything and if you feel you must walk away from me then I will understand and I will be able to join my son as there will be no reason for me to stay here.

I'm very, very sorry for this Linda. I feel that it's best for me not to write again after you have the statement from your brief.

I love you like I have done since that day I held you at the Old Bailey and I always believed I would overturn this sentence.

You must understand I totally believed what Gonzo told me about Ron and what he was doing to you. I did it out of love for you because you was there for me when my son died.

My love for you will never change. Now you will understand why I've been tortured so much.

My love is true

Yours always

Danny

xxxxxxx

The tape recording sent to me was made a month later on 6 November 2001. The following is the transcript:

I got a letter today from someone I used to respect. He was my friend but someone who told me a pack of lies. He didn't have the bottle to do something himself. Oh fucking hell. I went and got myself in a right fucking position.

Well about Linda – the lovely Linda, eh? What can you say about Linda? She is absolutely beautiful. I don't mean just to look at. If anyone knows Linda she is beautiful and honourable. If she is your friend she is your friend forever. She will stand by you no matter what; she would not let anyone say anything bad about ya. She will always stick up for ya.

She was my friend and she still is my best friend.

She was my friend long before we became romantically linked together. I never knew anything about Linda or her reputation. I never knew nothing about it.

We had a joke between us 'cos when her husband was shot dead I was in some pub and they came round for a collection for him. Someone just said to me that a bloke had been shot by the Old Bill. I put in £50 for him. Linda always said I should have brought the £50 round to her. We would have been together then. Not twenty years later.

I first met Linda in Brixton. In the visiting hall. She was there visiting Brian Thorogood. My mum was visiting me. I remember this woman walking in with a big fur coat on. You could see it was an expensive coat. She took it off and just slung it on the side. She had a top on with diamond sequins all over it.

I looked at her. She looked at me. We looked at each other – in the eyes.

She reminded me of one of those big horses – you know, one of those big powerful and proud horses – the way she was standing there. What a lovely looking woman, you know.

That was the first time I met Linda. Years later I told her what I felt when I saw her – when I saw her throw that coat over the table. She remembered it and laughed. She said she looked at me and told me what she thought. But none of us told each other until years and years later.

When she got her seven years I wrote to her from Wandsworth and told her I was gutted to hear that she got put down because I thought she was gonna get off, you know. Then she wrote back and said she was sorry that I got fourteen years. She understood about things more than I could imagine. Then we became friends from there.

Thorogood was in the same prison – Frankland. Linda used to write to him and that. She also used to write to me once a week and I used to call her my big sister. She was always getting silly girls to write to me from prison. But I wasn't interested.

That was when I really saw Linda, not in a romantic way, but I knew she was special. She was special to me.

When my son died I remember the first letter I got. It was from Linda. The first visit I got was from Linda. She used to go to the cemetery where my son was buried and put flowers on his grave every week for me because I couldn't do it. No one else would do that for me. Just her. There was a special bond between us. I used to feel it after that on our visits – the closeness – there was a bond between us.

All the time someone had told me something that I believed. And that weekend. I only went home that weekend to die – to go to the cemetery and do myself in. Which is why I sat there for two nights with a gun in my mouth. But for some reason I just couldn't fucking do it. I don't know why. I wasn't scared. I just couldn't fucking do it. I think my son was stopping me from doing it. Oh, I don't know.

So I did something else.

Linda has always believed that I'm as innocent as her. She is innocent.

I know that more than anybody because I'm the person that blew Ronnie Cook's head off.

I saw Linda standing in the corner with her hands over her face. She would never have known it was me. All that bollocks in the court that she should have identified me – not even my mother could have identified me. I had a wig on which was long. I had a false beard, like stubble – you know – designer thing. And a hat pulled down very low. That's why no one picked me out.

The park-keeper didn't even pick me out. I spoke to him. I asked him where the toilet was. He told me it was broken. He didn't pick me out. The copper didn't pick me out. He saw me sitting in the fucking park. No one picked me out. The woman next door is convinced to this day that it wasn't me. So how the fuck was Linda gonna pick me out when she was standing in the corner with her hands over her fucking face?

I've never told her. How could I tell her?

Fucking hell it's just one big nightmare that's gone wrong.

I wanted to plead guilty at my trial but Linda said I was just pleading guilty to get her out of trouble. There was no way she would accept that I did it. Well she was a bit confused 'cos I was in the area. Her mate's fucking brother took me to the area. He didn't know what I done. I told him I was going to see my first wife and son 'cos they live right there.

My mate was waiting. He dropped me off. I done what I did and I've denied it ever since because I've always believed that I would overturn this conviction because they based the conviction on lies. Complete lies.

So . . . I don't know what to do now. It's just all so confusing now because I believed what I was told – that Ronnie Cook used to beat her up and torture her. And after she done that – being there for me and my son – it was a pleasure to do it. I thought I was doing her a favour. Now, when she finds out . . . I don't know . . . where the future will be for me now. I don't think she will believe it. She will say that I'm just saying it now to get her out of trouble because that's how Linda is.

I suppose you think it's a bad thing, eh? How can I do anything else? I don't know.

I'm gonna write to my solicitors and say it may be the end of us.

You ask why I married her. I married her because I love her. I still love her and I'll always love her. There is a power between us. It's frightening. It's unbelievable. All we've had in the last twelve years is me and her. We've lived more together than people that are together outside. That sounds stupid doesn't it? But we have.

We write to each other every day. We have done for twelve years. Every day.

I backed out of the first marriage because of what I did. How could I marry her when she thinks I'm innocent like her – when I'm the man that done it? I'm the man, really, why she is in prison.

I've tried to take my life a few times, you know. They thought it was because of my son. But it was not only because of my son. It was because of being in prison. They are gonna say I'm just saying this now because we lost the case so we are stuck with it.

And now I get this fucking letter from Thorogood telling me he told me a pack of lies. So it was all for nothing. Ronnie Cook was not torturing her. I killed him and I went to prison for twelve years.

Me killing him fucked up Linda. I done it in her house. But I mean who would really think that Linda would be part of that – having it done in her own house? I mean that's where I thought we were gonna get a not guilty 'cos it was so absurd. She ain't gonna be part of that in her own house.

The Old Bill must have hated Linda 'cos they killed her husband and she stood up for him. She is magnificent. I have a thousand tons of respect for her. She is so honourable.

I don't know what is going to happen to our future. I really don't know. We will always be together me and Linda or my son. That's all I think about really, other than her.

I don't care about anybody around me. I never have done. I don't worry about what people think. I know all the things I've done. I've never back-stabbed any of my friends. They have all fucking stabbed me in the back. All of them. I'd die for my friends. Fucking hell. I bet this is a shock for you. I bet you never imagined you would get this did ya?

It's the truth. What a fucking mixed up way to be. It must have been fate. If I hadn't killed Ronnie Cook I wouldn't have been in prison. Linda wouldn't have been in prison. She probably still would be with Ronnie Cook now. And we wouldn't have been together now would we?

I wouldn't have not wanted to be together like we have been. I feel like I'm with someone who loves you totally, you know, one hundred per cent, that is always there for ya. It's a wonderful feeling.

Linda's saying is: 'You can't put a wedge where there is no gap.'

We are like twins – Siamese twins – me and Linda. I can feel it when she is not feeling right. I just know. I tell her in a letter and she does the same to me. It's frightening. It really is frightening.

She will know that I've been lying to her all these years. Not about love. You can't lie about love. You can't force yourself to love someone and you can't stop loving someone. So I have always loved her no matter what happened. And it was me who kicked in her front door and killed her boyfriend.

I have to laugh 'cos I thought we'd all walk out but I know I'll never walk out. I'll probably die in here now. But if they refer the case again and I'm put on the spot I'd do it again. I ain't bothered.

She has been in prison for fuck all. And I've had to sit and watch it. And all the time she thinks I've been in prison for fuck all too. I don't know what's going to happen now and how she is going to deal with this. I wish I could see her and talk.

Linda is my sun in the sky. She is everything. Each day I get her letter it lifts me up. I smell her letters. I read them over and over again, four, five, six times. I send her tapes and I take her everywhere all around the world and on the Orient Express and make love to her all round the world you know. And she has done the same to me. We love each other so much to get us through these last twelve years.

I saw her last night for the first time in a year. They could have kept us apart for ten years and it would not make the slightest bit of difference. We were sitting beside each other and the power between us just flows. It's like being boosted right up. Fucking hell I love Linda completely, I really do. I've never known anyone like her. I know she will forgive me because we cannot live without each other. I can't live without her and she can't live without me. I don't think there is anything that can turn us away from each other. I suppose I'll find out. Fucking hell.

I don't know whether this will help her or not. You know what these people are like – well, not these people – the courts. We'll just have to see. I can tell you hand on my heart the only reason I married Linda is because I love her. If I didn't love her I wouldn't have married her.

I don't just love her I worship her. She is my heroine. She's like a queen. When we are together it's magical.

So, what are we to make of this astonishing development? Why has it taken twelve years for this confession to emerge, and what made Brian Thorogood reveal his lies to Danny Reece now?

Both men admit to their enduring love for Linda Calvey and a cynic might say that this is the latest and most dramatic example of the hypnotic power she wields, even from behind bars, over the men who fall beneath her spell. Have they simply been lured once more into the Black Widow's web?

Danny Reece's belief that he and Linda are connected through some form of extra-sensory perception may not be so fanciful after all. Recently Linda told me of her own somewhat spooky psychic experiences.

'I had almost forgotten,' she said, 'but when I was young a fortune-teller told me that I would be married three times. My first two husbands would be killed and then I would marry a younger man. I know Ronnie was never my husband, but he treated me as his common-law wife so I suppose that counts. And certainly Danny is a much younger man. Isn't that weird?'

She went on to tell me how she had experienced premonitions over the deaths of both Micky Calvey and Ronnie Cook.

'I remember about three weeks before Micky died, I had a nightmare and I turned over violently in bed. As I did so I scratched Micky and drew blood. He got very cross but I apologised and told him that I had just dreamed that he was going to die in the street. "That's nice, innit?" he said, turned over and went back to sleep.

'Years later, when I was visiting Ron in prison, I went to cuddle him and suddenly I felt all cold and shivery. He asked me what was wrong and I told him that I had been overcome with a premonition that he would be killed and I would do time for it. "Don't be silly Princess," he said, and kissed me on the forehead.'

It was the end of the fortune-teller's prediction for Linda which I found intriguing: 'She said she saw me walking up a red carpet with dozens of photographers' flashguns going off all round me. Then from the crowd a woman fires a shot which hits me in the left arm.'

She looked at me with a deadly serious expression and said: 'That could be anybody's wife.'

Danny Reece faces his incarceration with a mixture of rage and depression. The conditions of his imprisonment vary between medical and psychiatric treatment to prevent suicide and solitary confinement after another bout of destructive fighting and vandalism. Meanwhile, Linda faces each day with a stoical calmness, convinced she will prove her innocence at any time. Her approach to prison authorities is based on this belief, as she explains in a typical anecdote:

The pettiness among some prison officers never ceases to amaze me, particularly those who are responsible for security.

Recently, when I had to go out of the prison to hospital for a check-up on my knee, the security officer who went with me insisted on tightening the handcuffs until they were biting into my wrists and were really quite painful.

I said to him: 'You are a sadist.' But he replied: 'No. I am the person who is responsible for making sure that you don't escape.'

He seemed incapable of recognising that, if you are going to escape, one more notch on the handcuffs is not going to stop you.

At the end of the day, of course, innocent people don't run away. Innocent people stay to prove their innocence don't they? One day that is exactly what I will do. I'm sure of it.

Well, we shall see.

If Reece's confession is believed, and is capable of convincing proof, then the Court of Appeal could yet quash Linda's conviction.

If Reece is not believed, ironically, he could be released before Linda Calvey. The Parole Board is always reluctant to release lifers who refuse to admit to the crime for which they have been convicted, while those who confess are invariably freed at the end of their tariff. The tariff will be spent next year.

Linda says: I just want to go home and be with my kids and my grandchildren. Of course I have forgiven Danny. What he did, he did for me. It just shows how much he truly loves me. It was murder. It was treachery. And it was all for a lie. How sad.'

INDEX